Seriously Good
BARBECUE
Cookbook

Seriously Good
BARBECUE
Cookbook

Over **100** of the
Best Recipes in the World

by *New York Times* Best-Selling Author
Brian Baumgartner
The Office

FOX CHAPEL
PUBLISHING

ISBN 978-1-4971-0475-4

Library of Congress Control Number: 2024936484

Photo Credits
Shutterstock.com: Used throughout: abuzayd (recipe servings), Mark Carrel (background), Pavlo
S (bottom flames); Krasovski Dmitri (background 3, 8); PanuShot (5); Pixel-Shot (grilled corn 9,
129); Sean Locke Photography (10); Katherine Welles (barbeque pit 11); Mr Doomits (pig sign
11); Wirestock Creators (barbeque 14); gowithstock (spoons of spices and herbs 17); The Toidi
(food thermometer 17); Timolina (tools 17); Romolo Tavani (top flames 18); RossHelen (grilling
18); julie deshaies (pork shoulder 19); Teri Virbickis (ribs on grill 19); Natasha Breen (20); Elena
Veselova (23); Foodio (25); F Armstrong Photography (28); Andrei Iakhniuk (38); xpixel (spices 41,
48, 71, 115, 143); hlphoto (47); Dar1930 (58); Elena Shashkina (sliced pork belly 63); Ivelin Denev
(chili 66); MaraZe (onions and spices 26, 66, 145); Pairoj Sroyngern (chili flakes 68, 145, 148);
Breaking The Walls (wooden scoop 73, 95, 149); VasiliyBudarin (ribs 73); stock creations (76); Nata
Bene (88); budihartono1 (ribs with bun 99); Tatiana Volgutova (102); Romix Image (oysters 106);
virtual studio (cinnamon sticks 106); Zyabich (kebabs 108); The Image Party (110); RFondren
Photography (120); rocharibeiro (campfire beans 124); New Africa (scoop 125); Nattika (green
beans 138); FoodAndPhoto (140); D_M (red peppers 144); Elena Veselova (BBQ sauce 145);
Shaiith (150); Ground Picture (158); Goskova Tatiana (lemonade 162); Kristi Blokhin (strawberry
daquiri 163); Larissa Bahr Photography (Brian photos: cover, 20) ; David Fisk, illustrations
throughout

To learn more about the other great books from Fox Chapel Publishing,
or to find a retailer near you, call toll-free
800-457-9112 or visit us at *www.FoxChapelPublishing.com.*

We are always looking for talented authors.
To submit an idea, please send a brief inquiry to
acquisitions@foxchapelpublishing.com.

Printed in Canada
First printing

ACKNOWLEDGMENTS

I want to acknowledge all of the hardworking people who worked tirelessly to make this cookbook a reality:

- David Miller, Gretchen Bacon, Elizabeth Martins, David Fisk, Matthew Hartsock, Diana Kern, Joseph Borden, Mike Deppen and all of the folks at Fox Chapel Publishing.
- Ted Gekis, Megan Smith, Ryan Zachary, Daniel Ribera, and Megan Dunn from my team.
- Paul Castrataro and Dylan Chant for their help. To the chefs and fans who contributed recipes: THANK YOU.
- And finally—a huge thank you to my friends and family who have tasted more barbecue over the last year than anyone thought possible. This could not have happened without YOU!

FOREWORD

In film and TV fandom, actors are often compared with their roles. Some seem to walk hand-in-hand with their on-screen personas, as though their character was written specifically with them in mind. Others bear little-to-no resemblance to those they portray, shocking fans during interviews with bookish shyness or a surprise British accent. Brian Baumgartner might be the most shining example of an actor who couldn't have less in common with his most famous character, Kevin Malone. My memories of the lovable, bumbling oaf from *The Office* almost instantly dissolved when I shook his hand, so immediately apparent were his warmth, charisma, and intelligence. Instead of garnering laughs from unintentional blunders, his chaotic wit kept me in stitches as I tried desperately to keep it together while we filmed. It's a testament to his abilities as a performer, but even more striking was his knowledge of and passion for good food. It might be the single thing he has in common with Kevin Malone.

But while the latter might have settled for microwaved spray-cheese "nachos," Brian has a much higher calling in cuisine. In his first cookbook, *Seriously Good Chili Cookbook*, he cataloged 177 of the best chili recipes from around the world. Instead of simply aggregating solid-looking recipes, he studied the very art of chili, extolling its history and sampling steaming pots from across the nation. He told the stories of chili cookoff winners, prolific bloggers, storied authors, and family and friends alike. And he did it all with the respect, curiosity, and enthusiasm that comes with being a true lover of great food. Now, with *Seriously Good Barbecue Cookbook*, he pays tribute to some of the greatest barbecue chefs, sharing their methods and spilling their secrets (but not on the carpet). He imparts his own studious knowledge, delicious recipes, and sheer enthusiasm for the medium, giving depth and context to the world of barbecue. Whether the rack of ribs headed into the smoker is your first or fiftieth batch, there's a wealth of knowledge, humor, and flavor to be enjoyed in the following pages.

So, start cooking your way through the *Seriously Good Barbecue Cookbook* and wonder with bated breath what cuisine Brian will tackle next. Personally, I hope it's nachos—those spray-cheese things are in need of redemption—but no matter the subject, it'll be another *Seriously* enjoyable addition to your cookbook collection.

—*Andrew Rea*
Chef & Creator of *Binging with Babish*

TABLE OF CONTENTS

INTRODUCTION

I grew up in the South—Georgia, to be precise.

And while I love Southern California (and my adopted hometown of Scranton, Pennsylvania), I wouldn't give up my childhood for nothing.

In the South, there is nothing more important than the "4 Fs": Family, Friends, Food, and Football. On Saturday mornings in the fall, I would often load into my friend's car to make the roughly 70-mile drive to Athens from Atlanta to attend a University of Georgia Football Game. (Go Dawgs!) Some days, as we headed into town, we would stop at The Varsity—a nostalgic, fast-food restaurant that felt like something out of the 50's, even almost 50 years ago. (In point of fact, it opened in 1928 and the charm of the place is they clung to that history.) Those days were fun. The Varsity always felt like a special treat, serving up hamburgers and chili dogs to all the faithful Bulldog fans. But those days weren't my favorite.

My favorite days were the barbecue tailgating days. We would leave Atlanta before dawn and arrive in Athens as the sun came up to set up our camper and barbecue pit to start cooking. Some Saturdays, we would smoke pork shoulder (pork butt) to make delicious pulled pork sandwiches. Tri-tip, brisket, and (of course) baby back ribs were also common guests at the party. The food was delicious to be sure. But I think for me, even at a young age, it was about the process as much as the actual food.

A few weeks ago, I went to Jacksonville, Florida for the "World's Largest Outdoor Cocktail Party," aka the UGA/Florida Game. Though, to be clear, it could just as easily be called the "World's Largest Outdoor BBQ Tailgating Party." Adjacent to the stadium, there's an area called "RV CITY" where folks start setting up a whole week before the game. They bring tents and trailers and campers and RVs and start grilling. I visited the "City" while I was there. I did a remote segment with my pal, Ryan McGee, for SEC NATION/ESPN from the madness. But to be honest, I felt like an outsider. Not that people weren't nice . . . they were very kind and generous. But there was something I missed. I thought about it long into the afternoon that day . . . Why did I not feel a part of it? Well, what I concluded was this— there is something communal about the process of barbecue and grilling and cooking for large numbers. It binds you together. Whatever your team. Whatever your politics. Whatever your background. Getting your hands dirty and making barbecue with folks (even sharing with strangers) is just about the most special way to bond.

I talk about this is terms of chili as well: "Nobody makes a pot of chili for just themselves." It's meant to be shared. Experienced together. Experimented with as you develop your own recipe with others. And while in my adulthood, chili has become what I'm known for, my true passion is grilling and barbecuing.

There's nothing better than spending a day tinkering over a grill, finding just the right flavor for just the right meat for just the right occasion. I don't have any particular allegiance. I love the tangy mustard of Carolina to the spicy red of Texas to the distinct, bold flavor of Memphis. I make it all, I eat it all, and this book is a collection of it all. I'm not serious about much, but I AM serious about barbecue.

How serious am I? In 2020, I drove over 700 miles across three states during a global pandemic to visit my folks. And while I was anxious to see them, as it had been nine months, I also had a place I needed to visit. I had seen a documentary feature about Rodney Scott and his barbecue restaurant in Charleston, South Carolina. Rodney, and a fellow by the name of Nick Pihakis, had started a joint out of "their mutual respect for the time and technique required to make great barbecue." The dying art of whole hog barbecue is what inspired them, and I wanted to view it and taste it for myself.

The circumstances were not ideal. I had to eat outdoors in roughly 95-degree heat while mostly wearing a mask and staying "socially distanced," but what I witnessed and ate was incredible. It was like watching a great artist work with preparation and technique mixed with improvisation and feel. The flavor profile was intense with juicy sumptuous meat . . . I could have watched them work and eaten their food all day long. And I almost did. It inspired me and from that moment on, I knew I needed to search for recipes and techniques and put them into a collection. Not just for others, but for myself!

I encourage you all to try different recipes. Get out of your comfort zone and explore not only different meats and sides, but also flavors. If you've never tried Carolina barbecue, try some, and as always, explore as you go. It's not scientific—these recipes are meant to be tinkered with and made better!

But most importantly, enjoy these recipes with others! Spend a day making something new with your friends and family. I promise you, you will not be disappointed. The food will be delicious, but the sense of community formed by cooking with and for others will make you fall in love with barbecue even more. I'm serious.

Cheers,

Brian Baumgartner

HOW THIS BOOK WAS MADE

It all started when I drove over 2,000 miles across the country to visit my parents. As I mentioned in the Introduction, I had to make a stop at Rodney Scott's BBQ in Charleston, South Carolina, but I had the whole country to drive through first! Rodney's and my parents' house—of course I couldn't forget them—were my destination(s), but in the meantime, I knew I wanted to stop in as many barbecue hubs as I could, even if I had to take a bit of a detour. I drove and ate my way east—beef brisket in Texas, burnt ends in Kansas City, pork ribs in Memphis, and a pulled pork sandwich in North Carolina. Finally, I turned south to head to the long-awaited and much-anticipated Rodney Scott's BBQ. While everything I savored along the way was revolutionary, that meal at Rodney's was an experience, and it sparked an idea.

If you know me, you know I'll stop at nothing to find the best of the best when it comes to food. First, I conquered chili, scouring the US and beyond for the best bowls I could get my hands on. This time, it would be barbecue. I couldn't stop thinking about everything that makes it so special—the art form, the aroma, the different styles, the unique twists, the people, all of it. I saw it and experienced it firsthand on my road trip across America, and it was a beautiful thing. I've always loved barbecue, but now I wanted to do something to show my appreciation for the best food on earth, and what better way to do that than with a cookbook?

So, just like chili, I was ready to embark on another endeavor to find the best barbecue recipes in the world, only this time, I wouldn't kiss my family goodbye and trek over mountains or through deserts like before. I decided to keep it simple. . .

I bought highway billboards. I designed newspaper and magazine ads. I got on podcasts. I took over local news stations and talk shows. I directed, produced, and aired prime-time commercials. I bought out entire media companies and TV networks. (Just kidding, I didn't do that . . .but I thought about it!) I hired pilots to write in the sky; others to fly banner ads over beaches. I drove through neighborhoods with a giant megaphone. I commandeered electronic traffic signs and vinyl-wrapped cars and trucks. I hired a pyrotechnic engineer to design some fireworks, and another guy to coordinate intricate drone light shows. I did absolutely everything I could to get the word out to any and all barbecue chefs that I wanted them.

And they answered the call!

From competitive barbecue champions to self-taught home cooks, people of all ages and from all walks of life were ready and willing to share their tried-and-true recipes. Because that's another thing that makes barbecue so special—there's plenty to go around.

I was blown away by the response and was eager to enter phase two: recreating their recipes to find the best 100. And boy, what a smoking good time it was. All good things take time and barbecue takes a lot of it, but I was ready to commit. I pitched a tent in my backyard to be closer to my grill and not disturb my wife in the wee hours. I labored over my smoker, basking in the glory to come. I coddled every recipe, nurturing each one like a newborn baby. Days went by, then weeks, then months. I was so consumed by meat that I had no idea what year it was by the time I was finally finished making every single recipe I had been given.

Not only was it fun, but it was a treat trying such a wide variety of barbecue—from Kansas City-Style Brisket Burnt Ends (page 34), Authentic Central Texas Brisket (page 40), and Memphis BBQ Chicken (page 67) to Vietnamese BBQ Pork Skewers (page 101), Joojeh Kababs (page 94), Pinchos de Pollo (page 96), and so many more. From the American South to the California coast and beyond to international cuisines, narrowing down the recipes was nearly impossible, but I knew it had to be done.

I decided to include a little bit of everything so there would be something for everyone. While there are plenty of traditional barbecue recipes (though maybe not in official competition categories) within these pages, you'll also find unique rubs, sauces, and marinades, tasty sides and appetizers, delicious desserts, seafood dinners, gluten-free options, and even boozy (and non-boozy) drinks! My goal was to make a go-to barbecue cookbook you can draw inspiration from, but also use to party plan and please a crowd of all ages. Luckily, some upstanding citizens read my mind and submitted everything I was looking for. And I have to admit, enjoying BBQ Oysters (page 106), followed by a Strawberry-Rhubarb Crumble (page 154), and washing it all down with a Lavender Lemonade (page 162) felt like the perfect finishing touch to round out the collection of recipes for this cookbook.

We had done it again.

So, without further ado, let's fire up the grill and get smoking. Starting with some of my very own recipes, it is my hope you find something you love, try it, and then experiment by adding your own personal touch. After all, that's how barbecue evolved and became what it is today all over the world!

Enjoy, fellow barbecue buffs!

MORE INFO HERE!

Throughout the book, you'll find some fun cooking videos to help bring this book to life. When you come across a QR code, simply open the camera on your phone or device, scan the code, and a link will appear for you to click and watch. Scan this code to go to all of the videos on the *Seriously Good Barbecue Cookbook* page!

ALL ABOUT BARBECUE

When we think of barbecue, it's pretty likely that the big four US regional styles come to mind first: Texas, Carolina, Kansas City, and Memphis. You might also think "America!", but barbecue stretches all across the globe, and way (and I mean way) further back in time. Before we dive into its history, let's allow its formal definition to set the stage:

> ## Bar•be•cue: verb
> 1. to roast or broil (food, such as meat) on a rock or revolving spit over or before a source of heat (such as hot coals or a gas flame)
> 2. to prepare (food, such as beef, pork, or chicken) by seasoning (as with a marinade, a barbecue sauce, or a rub) and cooking usually slowly and with exposure to low heat and to smoke
>
> Source: Merriam-Webster

1526:
The word "barbacoa" was written for the first time by Spanish explorer and historian Gonzalo Fernández de Oviedo y Valdés.

1540:
Spanish explorer Hernando de Soto and the Chicksaw tribe cooked the first barbecue feast together in modern-day Mississippi.

1650s:
One of the first laws passed in the colony of Virginia made the discharge of guns at a barbecue illegal.

1769:
George Washington references going to "Alexandria for a barbecue" and "staying all night" in his diary.

BARBECUE

MAN MEETS FIRE

We're talking the earliest days of human history and, yup, that means cavemen. Once they discovered fire, the rest really was history. Cooking their food over open flames was essentially how barbecue was born. (To try it yourself, see page 61 for a caveman-style recipe!) While there's a lot of debate, the barbecue we know and make today in the US began in the Caribbean—cooking meat over a grill with spices and sauces—and is also where the word "barbecue" comes from: barbacoa. The first known recording of "barbacoa" on paper appeared in 1526, written by a Spanish explorer, and thus began its "official" history.

BARBECUE ARRIVES IN AMERICA

The Spanish explorers who arrived in the Caribbean and witnessed this method of cooking took it with them on their continued expeditions. They traveled north and in 1540, close to present-day Mississippi and along with the Chicksaw tribe, they cooked a giant pork feast. From there, the technique snaked its way up through the colonies.

OUTSIDE INFLUENCE

As for all the varying regional styles? Well, let's just say there was a lot of influence and innovation from all over the place. Adding vinegar-based sauces to pork (North Carolina style) came from the British, who were partial to tart flavors. Using mustard-based sauces (South Carolina) was in thanks to the French and German settlers and their cultural preferences. (Dijon mustard and bratwursts anyone? It adds up.) Moving west, the Germans who settled in Texas were raising cattle, which introduced a new animal, giving pork a break. In Memphis, the easy access to molasses, which chefs mixed with tomato-based sauces, introduced a sweeter kind of barbecue. And by the early 1900s, a man named Henry Perry from Memphis moved to Kansas City, opened a restaurant, and began using his sweet-and-spicy Memphis roots to cook all kinds of meats instead of just pork, thus creating another regional style. And there you have it; how the big four schools of barbecue began.

TIMELINE

JULY 4, LATE 1700s:
Barbecues on this day became an annual party to celebrate America's victory in the Revolutionary War.

1878:
A butcher shop in Bastrop, Texas releases the first recorded advertisement to the public selling barbecue.

1921:
The first charcoal briquet factory was designed by Thomas Edison and built by Henry Ford.

1920s:
Bob Gibson invents the iconic Alabama white sauce, which he served over smoked chicken.

AIN'T NOTHING LIKE A BARBECUE PARTY

As is obvious, barbecue has long been a favorite American pastime. George Washington was especially fond of cookouts—his diary teemed with them, including a mention of a barbecue that lasted for days! Major American milestones—including when we won the Revolutionary War, built significant bridges, and laid the first foundational cornerstone of the Capitol building—were all celebrated afterward by way of barbecues.

A WORLD FULL OF BARBECUE

It's important to note that while barbecue is an American favorite, it by no means is exclusive to the US of A, of course. Nearly every country has been doing it for generations and takes pride in how they do it (something you'll get a taste of within these pages, even if it's just a small portion). Because it's so globally widespread, I could be here all day attempting to capture every amazing international barbecue style and how they came to be. But the one thing I will say is how wonderful it is that food, barbecue in particular, can bring all of us together. We all do it differently, but we also all have it in common and are more than happy to swap notes.

SHARING IS CARING

I hope you will have as much fun as I did recreating these delicious dishes. Whether you stick with a favorite style, a classic go-to, or branch out and discover something new, barbecue is all about community—as long as you serve up these meals surrounded by good company, you're doing it right.

BARBECUE ESSENTIALS

From pantry essentials to grilling tools, the following are must-haves when it comes to BBQ. I could go on and on with this list, but to keep things simple, this is a great place to start for beginners:

PANTRY

- **Pure Vegetable Oil/Cooking Oil Spray.** This is essential for lubricating meat and grill grates.

- **Kosher or Sea Salt.** The larger crystals of kosher or sea salt are wonderful because you can actually see where you have salted.

- **Garlic (granulated and fresh).** This is a basic flavor for most grilling sauces and rubs.

- **Cumin.** This is the secret spice of all great barbecue cooks.

- **Onions (powdered, granulated, or fresh).** Onions enhance most every barbecue recipe.

- **Apple Cider Vinegar.** This provides the flavor of apple cider without the sugar and is the choice of most master grillers. Use by itself as a spray or as a liquid component of wet rubs, mops, and sauces. It's also great for soaking your wood chips before you use them.

- **Ketchup.** This versatile ingredient is perfect for forming a quick sauce and plays well with other ingredients.

- **Brown Sugar.** Great for dry rubs. When combined with ketchup, it creates a sweet glaze for pork or chicken. I even sprinkle a touch on steaks.

EQUIPMENT

- **Knives.** A quality knife is essential to prepping and carving meat. Choose one that feels good in your hand, can work for different tasks, can be used outdoors, doesn't cost a fortune, and are easy to clean and sharpen.

- **Spatula.** Find one with a wooden handle and a sturdy blade that supports a good-sized steak that can easily slide between the grate and the food.

- **Tongs.** Tongs come in a variety of colors to indicate their purpose. I use red ones for raw meat and black ones for meat that's cooked.

- **Fork.** They come in handy with tongs and a spatula when a little extra help is needed. Never use it to poke or turn meat.

- **Basting Brush.** A silicone cooking utensil is crucial. The angle is great for getting to hard-to-reach places, and the brush holds sauce and clarified butter really well.

- **Thermometers.** Instant-read thermometers are very useful for quickly testing meat in various areas to see if it's cooking evenly.

- **Heat-Resistant Leather Gloves.** These are intended for heavy industrial use and can take sparks, heat, and hot metal. They are very useful when you need to move hot grates and cast iron pans, and when working around your grill, smoker, or barbecue.

ALL ABOUT HEAT

The roots of modern grilling go back to prehistoric times when our ancestors placed a chunk of meat on a stick and held it in the fire. Judging by the number of people who love outdoor cooking today, there's something in the way the intense heat crisps the meat's surface that still appeals to our deeply rooted DNA.

While we've refined the caveman's cooking tools and techniques a bit over the ensuing eons, there are certain things that haven't changed. The most important of these is the management of heat. This is probably the most basic skill required of any good cook, whether they're preparing a meal in the kitchen or the backyard. But because this book is about outdoor cooking, let's start with some basic facts about the heat we use to grill, barbecue, and smoke food.

In outdoor cooking, the heat source we use most often is fire. Whether its source is the propane in a gas grill, the charcoal in a smoker, or the logs on a campfire, fire produces heat; and we can harness that heat to cook foods to our delight. Fire requires three things to burn: combustible material, a supply of oxygen, and a source of ignition. There are many materials that can burn; yet only a few—such as wood, charcoal, and propane or natural gas—are suitable for cooking food.

Outdoor cooking enthusiasts often refer to heat as either **direct** or **indirect**. The most popular form of **direct heat** cooking is **grilling**, which means cooking food directly over the heat source, usually at high

HOT TIP

Barbecuing "low and slow" works best for large, less-tender cuts of meat, such as pork shoulder.

temperatures. We typically grill steaks, chops, burgers, and fish. We can also use a grill's **indirect heat** to cook food more slowly and at lower temperatures further away from the heat source. Whole chickens, briskets, roasts, and other large cuts of meat are usually cooked by this method, which we generally call **barbecuing**.

COOKING TECHNIQUES

Many people mistakenly refer to any type of cooking on their grill as "barbecuing," but that's not entirely correct. Shall we break down the differences of outdoor cooking techniques? I think we shall . . .

GRILLING

Grilling involves quickly cooking individual portions of food at relatively high temperatures over a direct heat source. The first step in many grilling recipes is to sear the meat over high heat—between 350°F to 550°F. The

higher heat browns the outside of smaller cuts of meat, sealing in juices that would be lost if the meat were cooked more slowly. My mother did this before placing a roast in the oven, and I do it every time I grill a steak. Cast-iron grates on a grill are also highly conductive, which significantly aids the searing process.

Once food is seared, you'll often finish cooking over indirect heat on another part of the grill. The reason food can continue to cook this way is that there's still plenty of heat generated by one or more of these sources: 1) **convective** heat from air heated by the fire; 2) **conductive** heat from the grill grates; and 3) **radiant** heat produced by either a charcoal or an infrared gas grill.

BARBECUING

Barbecuing is a slower way of cooking large portions of meat or poultry using an indirect source of heat at a lower temperature (usually between 225°F to 350°F). It takes time, but the end result is tender and juicy. Here's the science behind barbecue: when meat is placed away from the heat source, it cooks by "bathing" in the hot air—or convective heat—generated by the fire. Another way you might describe barbecuing is slow roasting at low temperatures. Cuts of meat that benefit from this type of cooking, such as pork shoulder and beef brisket, have a high ratio of collagen in the meat. (Translation: they're tough.) Slow cooking with indirect heat works magic on these cuts, breaking down the dense collagen and adding tenderness and flavor.

Talk to any long-time outdoor cooking enthusiast and sooner or later you're going to hear the phrase "low and slow." In fact, it's pretty much the official motto of all barbecue. "Low" refers to temperature—generally between 225°F to 350°F. "Slow" means the time it takes to cook the food. Simply stated, "Good eating comes to those who cook low and slow."

SMOKING

Smoking is the process of cooking food on or near an open fire made from materials such as wood or charcoal. The fire releases particles of these materials into the smoker that impart a unique flavor to the meat. The more these materials smolder and generate smoke, the greater the number of particles to flavor the food. Cooking at temperatures between 140°F–225°F is called **hot smoking.**

If the smoke passes through a cooling chamber and comes into contact with the food at a temperature of around 45°F, you are cold smoking the food. (Note: cold-smoked food isn't actually cooked; it's simply being slow-cured and flavored.)

When moisture is added to the smoker to increase its humidity level, it is called **wet smoking.** A simple pan of water is placed away from direct heat inside the grill or smoker. If desired, you can use fruit juice or wine instead of water, or add these liquids to the water for an additional flavor boost.

HOT TIP

Smoking with wood or charcoal on a charcoal grill uses indirect heat.

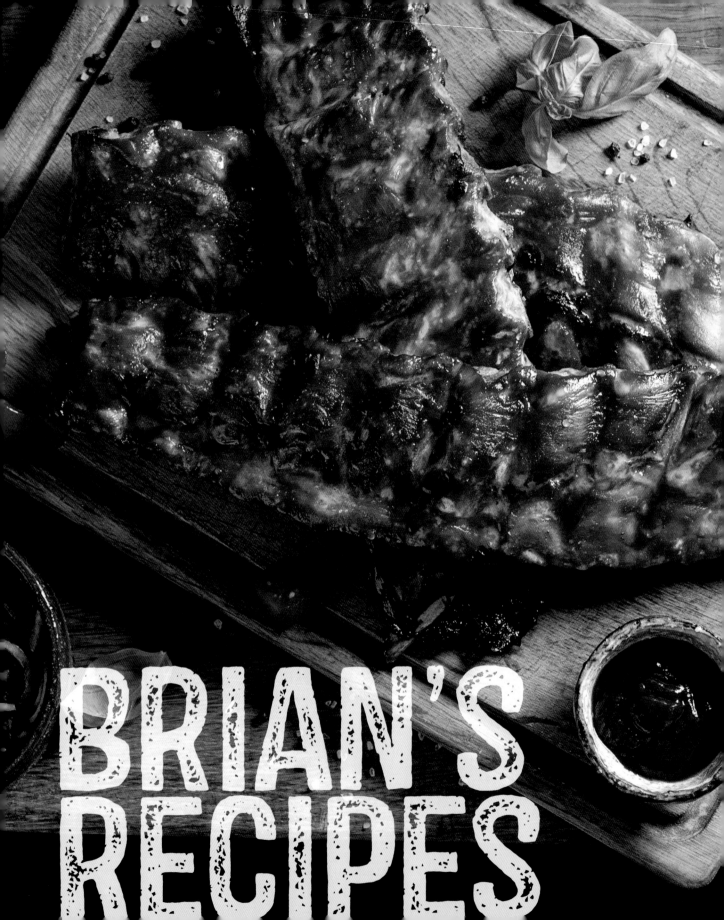

To kick things off, in this section, you'll find two of my very own go-to barbecue recipes that I've meticulously perfected over the years. I'm revealing all my secrets with these two recipes, so I hope you enjoy. You'll also find a simple yet seriously good barbecue recipe by renowned celebrity chef and social media darling, Nick DiGiovanni!

THE BEST GRILLED CHICKEN BREAST WITH WHIPPED GARLIC SAUCE

SMOKED BABY BACK RIBS

SPECIAL GUEST RECIPE

MOM'S BBQ CHICKEN

BEST GRILLED CHICKEN BREAST
WITH WHIPPED GARLIC SAUCE

SERVES 10

PREP TIME: 4 HOURS, 15 MINUTES | COOK TIME: 30 MINUTES

My favorite dish. I serve it almost once a week! Plus, this sauce can be stored safely for up to three months in the fridge!

INGREDIENTS

GRILLED CHICKEN:
- Ten 10–12-ounce boneless and skinless chicken breasts, or as many breasts as servings as you want (1 breast per serving)

HOMEMADE WHIPPED GARLIC SAUCE:
- 1 cup peeled garlic cloves
- 2 teaspoons kosher salt
- 3 cups safflower oil
- ½ cup lemon juice

HOMEMADE ITALIAN DRESSING:
- 1 cup extra virgin olive oil

- ½ cup red wine vinegar
- Juice from half a lemon
- 1 tablespoon sugar
- 1 tablespoon oregano
- ½ tablespoon dried basil
- ½ tablespoon organic onion powder
- 3 cloves fresh garlic, diced
- 1 teaspoon garlic powder
- ½ teaspoon salt
- ½ teaspoon pepper
- ¼ teaspoon celery salt
- 1 tablespoon grated parmesan cheese

DIRECTIONS

1. Preheat the grill to medium-high heat, about 400°F. (Make sure there is room on the grill for direct and indirect heat.)

HOMEMADE WHIPPED GARLIC SAUCE:
1. Combine the garlic and salt into a food processor and blend it completely until it's finely minced.
2. Continually scrape down the garlic from the sides to make sure all the garlic stays together.
3. With the food processor running, begin adding the oil, just a couple tablespoons at a time. Stop and scrape the sides. It's important to begin adding the oil slowly at first, scraping and combining the oil with the garlic until it becomes creamy.
4. Once the garlic looks emulsified by the few tablespoons of oil, increase the speed of pouring the oil and alternate with the lemon juice until all the oil and lemon juice is incorporated. This will take about 15 minutes to complete.
5. Transfer to a bowl with a lid and store in the fridge. Leaving overnight will give it a better flavor the next day.

HOMEMADE ITALIAN DRESSING:
1. Put all of the ingredients together in a bowl and stir to combine. It's that easy!
2. Marinate the chicken in the Italian dressing for 3–4 hours before cooking.

GRILLED CHICKEN:
1. Place the chicken on the grill over direct heat. Cover.
2. Leave the chicken on for 6–7 minutes, then flip.
3. Cook for another 6–7 minutes on the other side.
4. The chicken should have nice grill marks on each side. Remove the chicken from direct heat and move to an area in grill with indirect heat. Keep the temperature in the grill around 400°F and leave on for another 15 minutes. The chicken should stay moist but continue to cook through.
5. When it's done, remove and serve with Homemade Whipped Garlic Sauce.

HOT TIP

For speed or if you're in a pinch, I recommend using Majestic Garlic Sauce. It can be found at many natural food markets.

HOT TIP

For speed or if you're in a pinch, I recommend using Girard's Olde Venice Italian Dressing to marinate instead.

Picking Your Chicken

If you have access to a local farm or butcher, source your meat from them. Otherwise, I have found Smart Chicken to be the absolute best source for quality, fresh chicken; it stays moist and doesn't dry out.

MY SECRET

My secret to perfectly cooked meat? Use a combination of direct and indirect heat on the grill! I typically start with direct heat and then move meat to indirect heat to finish cooking. This allows the meat to cook through safely while not drying out.

SMOKED BABY BACK RIBS

SERVES 2

PREP TIME: 15 MINUTES | COOK TIME: 5–6 HOURS

Two racks of baby back ribs! Each rack will feed about two people, so increase the rub ratios and get more ribs if feeding more people!

INGREDIENTS

RIBS:
- 2 racks baby back ribs

RUB:
- 8 tablespoons sweet paprika
- 5 tablespoons brown sugar
- 3 tablespoons kosher salt
- 2 tablespoons black pepper, freshly ground
- 1 tablespoon ground cumin
- 2 tablespoons garlic powder
- 2 tablespoons onion powder
- 1 tablespoon mustard powder
- ½ teaspoon hot cayenne pepper

HOT TIP

The day before, soak the chips or pellets in apple cider overnight. This will give your ribs a delicious, sweet, and smoky flavor.

DIRECTIONS

RUB:
1. Combine the ingredients in a bowl and mix well.

RIBS:
1. Wash the ribs in cold water and pat dry. If possible, have your local butcher remove the membrane. If not, remove the membrane before continuing.
2. Liberally place rub all over the ribs.
3. Preheat your grill to 225°F. (I like to smoke my ribs with hickory chips.)
4. Place the ribs bone down on your smoker/indirect heat. Cooking time will vary, but expect the ribs to smoke for 5–6 hours. I like to put apple cider in a spray bottle and occasionally spray the ribs as they cook to keep them moist. It will also help the smoky flavor adhere to the ribs better. You can also spray the chips with apple cider to extend their life and replace chips with fresh soaked chips as you go if needed.
5. Test the ribs using the "bend method." Pick up one end of the rack and allow the ribs to bend. If the meat cracks and starts to separate, they are finished. The meat should not fall off the bone.
6. That's it! After the bones pass the bend test, let them rest for 20 minutes and serve as is, or with your favorite barbecue sauce!

HOT TIP

If you don't have a smoker, you can use your gas grill and a "Smoker Box." I recommend Weber's Universal Stainless Steel Smoker Box. Simply place the pre-soaked chips in the box over direct heat and place the ribs bone down on the other part of the grill.

The Best Tri-Tip

The best tri-tip I have ever had comes from Seaside Market in Cardiff-by-the-Sea, California. Their Burgundy Pepper Tri-Tip is so good, the locals call it "Cardiff Crack." This local market now ships their "Crack" coast to coast to those addicted to its unique, delicious flavor.

MOM'S BBQ CHICKEN

SERVES 4–6

COOK TIME: 50 MINUTES

Growing up, my mom used to make this delicious barbecue chicken recipe. There's no grill required . . . just an oven and a little patience! I've also added on my own twist of lemon zest, which brings a nice, bright addition.

INGREDIENTS

- 8 bone-in, skin-on chicken thighs
- 1 cup barbecue sauce of your preference
- Zest of 1 lemon
- Salt and pepper, to taste
- 2 tablespoons chopped fresh cilantro or parsley (optional, for garnish)

DIRECTIONS

1. Preheat your oven to 425°F and line a baking sheet with parchment paper.

2. Season both sides of the chicken with salt and pepper. Place the chicken in a bowl and cover with ½ cup of the barbecue sauce. Mix to combine and set aside while your oven heats.

3. Add the chicken to the baking sheet skin side down. Reserve any leftover barbecue sauce in the bowl. Bake the chicken for 25 minutes.

4. Flip the chicken over and drizzle the top with the barbecue sauce that was in the marinating bowl. Return to the oven and bake skin side up for another 20 minutes.

5. Turn your oven to a broil and position the oven rack accordingly. Baste the top of the chicken with the remaining ½ cup of barbecue sauce and broil for 3–5 minutes, or until the top is dark and caramelized.

6. Finish with finely grated lemon zest.

HOT TIP

Instead of a broiler, finish them off on a grill for extra char and flavor!

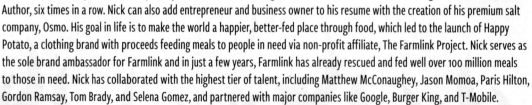

Nick DiGiovanni

Nick DiGiovanni is a chef, culinary content creator, social media megastar, and world record holder for numerous food-related feats. After becoming the youngest-ever finalist on *MasterChef*, Nick rapidly gained a loyal, eager-to-learn audience for his award-winning video content. Today, Nick has over 30 million followers across social media, has broken nine world records, has been honored by Forbes's 30 Under 30, and has won Streamy Awards and Webby Awards for his online content. In 2023, Nick released his first cookbook, *Knife Drop: Creative Recipes Anyone Can Cook*, becoming an instant *New York Times* Best-Selling Author, six times in a row. Nick can also add entrepreneur and business owner to his resume with the creation of his premium salt company, Osmo. His goal in life is to make the world a happier, better-fed place through food, which led to the launch of Happy Potato, a clothing brand with proceeds feeding meals to people in need via non-profit affiliate, The Farmlink Project. Nick serves as the sole brand ambassador for Farmlink and in just a few years, Farmlink has already rescued and fed well over 100 million meals to those in need. Nick has collaborated with the highest tier of talent, including Matthew McConaughey, Jason Momoa, Paris Hilton, Gordon Ramsay, Tom Brady, and Selena Gomez, and partnered with major companies like Google, Burger King, and T-Mobile.

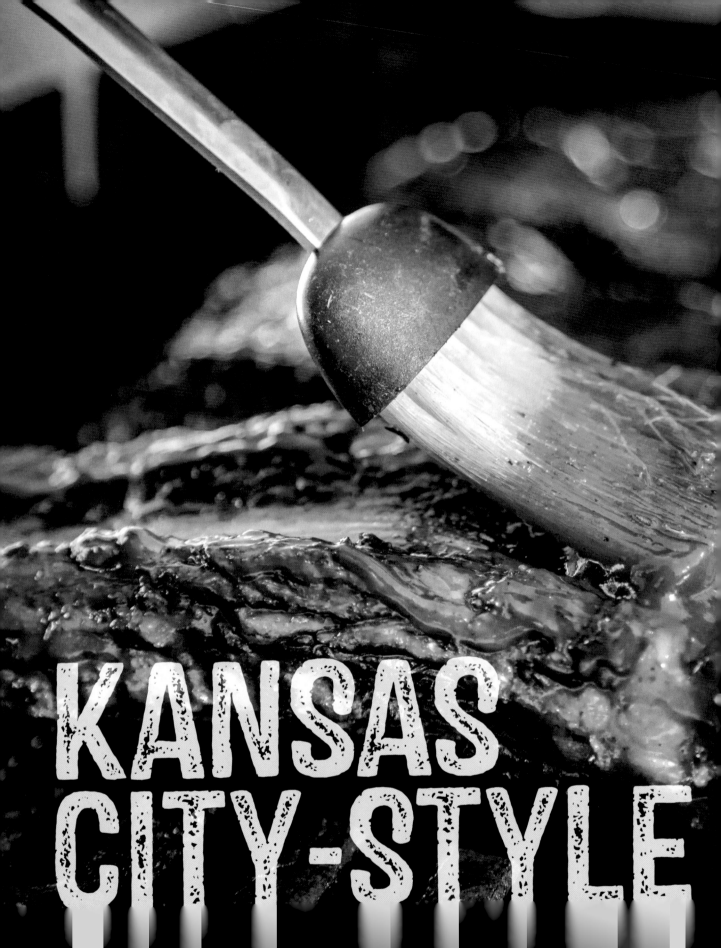

KANSAS CITY-STYLE

Nothing says Kansas City-style barbecue like a signature, ultra-thick, super sweet sauce that's loaded with brown sugar, molasses, and tomatoes, and meats slow-smoked to perfection. From the hallmark burnt ends to the quintessential meats like Kansas City ribs, brisket, and pulled pork, each dish is carefully prepared to prevent the caramelizing sugar from charring the meat, creating a sweet and savory combination emblematic of this iconic style. These recipes use those tried-and-true flavors and also offer unique twists on this renowned regional style.

CANDY PORK BELLY BURNT ENDS

KANSAS CITY BBQ CHICKEN LEGS

COMPETITION RIBS GLAZED WITH KANSAS CITY BBQ SAUCE

KANSAS CITY-STYLE BRISKET BURNT ENDS

SLOW-COOKED SWEET AND TANGY BBQ GLAZED CHICKEN

THE BEST BBQ CHICKEN DRUMSTICKS

CANDY PORK BELLY BURNT ENDS

SERVES 6

PREP TIME: 30 MINUTES | COOK TIME: 3 HOURS, 30 MINUTES

DYLAN ZIMMERMAN | RIO VISTA, CALIFORNIA

I came up with this recipe using the flavors I love to create a perfect balance of sweet and heat. It's a very simple recipe that someone new to barbecue can master. It's about a 3½-hour cook with just a couple simple tasks to complete it.

Soak Your Wood Chips

When grilling with wood chips, I like to soak the chips in apple cider for a day. It gives a sweet addition to the flavor of the wood.

INGREDIENTS

- 2 tablespoons olive oil
- 2 pounds pork belly
- ½ cup barbecue rub (I used Blazing Star BBQ Scorpion rub)
- 1 stick butter
- ½ cup brown sugar
- 2 tablespoons honey
- 1 cup barbecue sauce (I used Blazing Star BBQ Original Sauce)

DIRECTIONS

1. Cut your pork belly into 2-inch x 2-inch cubes.
2. Lightly drizzle with the olive oil and mix to coat. This will help the rub stick.
3. Season the cubes evenly on all sides with the barbecue rub. Set the cubes on a wire cooking rack.
4. Bring your smoker to a temperature between 250°F–275°F and add cherry wood for that smoky flavor.
5. When the smoker comes up to temperature, put the pork belly on. Spritz with water every 30 minutes until the pork belly gets a nice color and bark.
6. Around 2 hours, remove the pork belly and put in an aluminum pan. Add the butter, brown sugar, honey, and barbecue sauce.
7. Wrap the top of the pan in foil and put back in the smoker until the internal temperature reaches between 200°F–205°F, which will be about another an hour and a half.
8. Remove the pan from the smoker. Put the pork belly back on the wire cooking rack and place back on the smoker for 15 minutes to tack on the sauce.

KANSAS CITY BBQ CHICKEN LEGS

PREP TIME: 30 MINUTES | COOK TIME: 30 MINUTES

JENNIFER SIKORA | CALVERT CITY, KENTUCKY

I found this recipe to be a staple for our family when money was tight. Chicken legs are a cheaper cut of meat, meaning you can make more to feed more people when you're on a budget. This recipe comes together in less than 30 minutes and barbecue chicken legs are hands down my favorite thing to eat these days.

SERVES 7+

INGREDIENTS

BARBECUE SAUCE:
- 2 cups ketchup
- ⅓ cup regular molasses
- ⅓ cup brown sugar
- ⅓ cup apple cider vinegar
- 1 teaspoon garlic powder
- ½ teaspoon smoked paprika
- ½ teaspoon dry mustard
- ½ teaspoon ancho chili powder
- ½ teaspoon onion powder
- ½ teaspoon freshly ground black pepper
- ½ teaspoon salt
- 2 teaspoons liquid smoke

CHICKEN LEGS:
- 10–12 chicken drumsticks

DIRECTIONS

1. In a bowl, mix all the barbecue sauce ingredients together and place in a saucepan. Simmer for 15 minutes.
2. While the sauce is simmering, place the chicken legs on a pan and season with salt and pepper.
3. Once the sauce is done simmering, pour ½ cup of sauce into a bowl and reserve the rest to share with the family.
4. Heat the grill to medium heat. Spray with nonstick cooking spray.
5. Place the chicken legs on the grill.
6. Begin basting them with ½ cup of sauce. After 6 minutes, flip the chicken legs and baste the other side with the barbecue sauce.
7. Continue this pattern until the chicken legs are done. The thermometer will read 160°F internal temperature in the thickest part of the meat.

My Barbecue Must-Have

My favorite tools for grilling are my **Black Rain Pepper Mill** and my **White Rain Salt Mill**. They're so easy to use and provide fresh ground pepper and salt with a push of the button.

COMPETITION RIBS
GLAZED WITH KANSAS CITY BBQ SAUCE

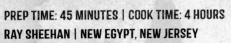
SERVES 6

PREP TIME: 45 MINUTES | COOK TIME: 4 HOURS

RAY SHEEHAN | NEW EGYPT, NEW JERSEY

Pork ribs rule the world . . . the barbecue world that is. Whether you aspire to be your neighborhood's rib king or compete on the professional barbecue circuit, these smoky, tender, pull-the-meat-from-the-bone ribs are the ones you'll want to serve. This recipe has helped us win many awards and top ten calls at barbecue events, both large and small.

INGREDIENTS

RIBS:

- Two 2½-pound slabs St. Louis–cut pork ribs
- ¼ cup prepared yellow mustard
- Sweet and Smoky BBQ Rub, as needed (ingredients and recipe below)
- Apple juice, for spritzing
- ½ cup honey
- 1 cup packed light brown sugar
- ¼ cup hot sauce
- ¼ cup (½ stick) unsalted butter, melted
- 1 cup Kansas City Barbecue Sauce, warmed (see ingredients and recipe)

SWEET AND SMOKY BARBECUE RUB:

- ½ cup light brown sugar
- 2 tablespoons sea salt
- 1 tablespoon smoked paprika
- 1 tablespoon granulated garlic
- 1 tablespoon onion powder
- 2 teaspoons freshly ground black pepper
- 2 teaspoons dry mustard
- ½ teaspoon ancho chili powder
- ½ teaspoon cayenne pepper

KANSAS CITY BARBECUE SAUCE:

- 2 cups ketchup
- ½ cup packed light brown sugar
- ⅓ cup molasses
- ¼ cup apple cider vinegar
- 2 tablespoons prepared yellow mustard
- 1 tablespoon Worcestershire sauce
- 2 tablespoons onion powder
- 2 teaspoons chili powder
- 1½ teaspoons granulated garlic
- 1 teaspoon freshly ground black pepper
- ¼ teaspoon cayenne pepper
- 2 teaspoons natural hickory liquid smoke

DIRECTIONS

1. Prepare a smoker to cook at 275°F.

SWEET AND SMOKY BARBECUE RUB:

1. In a small bowl, combine all of the rub ingredients. Mix well, then set aside. Any leftover rub may be stored in an airtight container for up to 6 months.

KANSAS CITY BARBECUE SAUCE:

1. In a medium-sized saucepan, combine all of the sauce ingredients and bring to a gentle boil over medium heat, stirring to dissolve the sugar.

2. Lower the heat to low and simmer, stirring occasionally, until slightly thickened, 5 to 8 minutes.

3. Remove from the heat, let cool, transfer to a jar, and store it in the refrigerator until ready to use. Leftover sauce can be stored in the refrigerator for up to a month.

RIBS:

1. Remove the membrane from the back of the ribs and trim away any excess fat. Remove the end bones from each slab to square them up.

2. Apply a thin coat of mustard to each side and sprinkle on an even layer of the rub to both sides of the ribs. Let them sit for 30 minutes to let the rub set up.

3. Once the cooker reaches temperature, place the ribs on the smoker and cook for 2½ hours, spritzing with apple juice after the first hour, then every 30 minutes.

4. Lay out two sheets of heavy-duty aluminum foil. Layer half of the honey, brown sugar, hot sauce and butter on each foil. Lightly dust these with some more of the rub and spritz them with apple juice.

5. Place each slab of the ribs, meat side down, on each honey mixture-topped sheet of foil and wrap up the foil packages tightly.

6. Place the wrapped ribs back on the pit and continue to cook for about an hour, then check the ribs for doneness by opening the packages and pushing a toothpick into the meat. It should go in and out easily. Continue to cook to your desired tenderness.

7. Once the ribs are done, remove from the smoker and open the foil to vent for about 15 minutes. This will prevent the ribs from further cooking.

8. Remove them from the foil and transfer the ribs to a sheet pan. Combine ¼ cup of the juices from the foil with the barbecue sauce and brush it onto both sides of the ribs to glaze. Place the ribs back on the smoker and cook for 15 to 20 minutes to set the glaze.

9. Remove the ribs from the cooker and allow them to rest for 5 minutes. Slice the ribs individually and arrange them on a platter to serve.

St. Louis-Style Ribs vs. Spareribs

What's the difference between St. Louis-style ribs and regular spareribs? Not much! The only difference is that St. Louis-style ribs are cut uniformly. All of the extra meat and bones along the top and on the sides of the ribs have been trimmed off. That's it!

KANSAS CITY-STYLE BRISKET BURNT ENDS

SERVES 7+

PREP TIME: 15 MINUTES | COOK TIME: 6+ HOURS

PAULA STACHYRA | TORONTO, ONTARIO, CANADA

My father has always been a grill enthusiast and loved to travel to different states that are known for barbecue to taste the different styles and methods of grilling and smoking. He fell in love with Kansas City barbecue, particularly the iconic brisket burnt ends. These crispy, flavorful, and succulent morsels had a character of their own, unlike anything he had tasted before. Since then, he's perfected his recipe for Kansas City-Style burnt ends that continue to captivate the taste buds of those who try them, including me. This recipe has been handed down to me from my dad. It's a true labor of love that can take up to 12 hours and it's worth every one.

INGREDIENTS

- One 4–6-pound brisket point
- 1 tablespoon yellow mustard
- ½ cup beef broth, for spritz
- ¼ cup honey
- 4 tablespoons unsalted butter, divided into small pats

KANSAS CITY-STYLE DRY RUB:

- ½ cup brown sugar
- ¼ cup paprika
- 1 tablespoon black pepper
- 1 tablespoon kosher salt
- 1 tablespoon chili powder
- 1 tablespoon onion powder
- 1 tablespoon garlic powder
- 1 teaspoon cayenne pepper
- 1 teaspoon dry mustard

KANSAS CITY-STYLE BARBECUE SAUCE:

- 2 cups ketchup
- ⅓ cup apple cider vinegar
- 2 tablespoons Worcestershire sauce
- 2 tablespoons honey
- 1 tablespoon smoked paprika
- 1 teaspoon dry mustard
- 1 teaspoon garlic powder
- 1 teaspoon onion powder
- 1 teaspoon chili powder
- ¼ teaspoon cayenne pepper
- Salt and pepper, to taste
- 1 tablespoon your favorite bourbon (optional)

DIRECTIONS

1. Preheat smoker to 250°F. Transfer the beef broth to a spray bottle.

2. If you have a whole packer brisket, separate the point from the flat by running a sharp knife through the hard, white fat between the two muscles. Trim any hard fat, tough pieces, remove any silver skin, and trim the top fat cap down to about ¼-inch thick.

3. In a small bowl, combine all of the Kansas City-Style Dry Rub ingredients.

4. Slather the brisket with the yellow mustard on both sides and season the brisket liberally on both sides.

5. Place the brisket point on the top shelf in the grill and smoke the brisket point for about 6–8 hours until it reaches an internal temperature of 165°F, spritzing with beef broth after 3 hours, or when there are dry spots on the meat, and then every hour or as needed. Note: Avoid spritzing too frequently, as this will add too much moisture on top of the meat and the desired bark will not form.

6. Meanwhile, prepare the Kansas City-Style Barbecue Sauce. In a large saucepan, combine the ketchup, apple cider vinegar, Worcestershire sauce, honey, smoked paprika, dry mustard, garlic powder, onion powder, chili powder, cayenne pepper, salt, pepper, and bourbon. Simmer over low heat for about 25 minutes, stirring occasionally. Let it cool and store in an airtight container or mason jar until you're ready to use it.

7. Once the brisket point reaches an internal temperature of 165°F, double wrap it tightly in pink butcher paper and return it to the grill. Smoke until the internal temperature reaches 190–195°F, about 2–3 more hours.

8. Remove the brisket point from the grill and unwrap it from the butcher paper, draining any liquid from the paper into an aluminum pan. Cut the brisket point into 1½-inch-thick cubes.

9. Place the cubes into the aluminum pan and toss with the Kansas City-Style Barbecue Sauce and honey, then top with the pats of butter.

10. Place the uncovered pan on the grill and smoke for 1–2 more hours, or until the burnt ends have absorbed the barbecue sauce and the sauce has thickened. The sauce should be sticky to the touch. Remove the pan from the grill and allow it to cool for about 10–15 minutes before serving.

SLOW-COOKED SWEET AND TANGY BBQ GLAZED CHICKEN

SERVES 6

PREP TIME: 15 MINUTES | COOK TIME: 4 HOURS
ELIZABETH MARTINS | PHILADELPHIA, PENNSYLVANIA

This Slow-Cooked Sweet and Tangy BBQ Glazed Chicken recipe is a crowd-pleaser, ideal for gatherings or family dinners. It uniquely balances tender chicken breasts with a rich blend of barbecue sauce, brown sugar, and Worcestershire sauce. What sets it apart is the omission of Italian dressing, replaced with a blend of olive oil and vinegar, allowing you to increase/emphasize a delightful vinegar undertone (if you wish). This twist, combined with the ease of crockpot cooking, results in a tender, flavorful dish perfect for sandwiches, salads, over rice, or simply by itself!

INGREDIENTS

- 2 pounds boneless skinless chicken breasts
- 1 cup barbecue sauce
- 2 tablespoons olive oil
- 2 tablespoons vinegar
- ¼ cup brown sugar
- 1 tablespoon Worcestershire sauce
- Salt, to taste

DIRECTIONS

1. Prepare your chicken breasts by cutting off any fat.
2. If your chicken breasts are on the thicker side, slice them in half so the juice can get inside the meat quicker!
3. Season each chicken breast with a small pinch of salt and rub it in.
4. Place chicken breasts in the slow cooker.
5. In a mixing bowl, combine the barbecue sauce, olive oil, vinegar, brown sugar, and Worcestershire sauce. Stir everything until it's nicely combined.
6. Pour the mixture over the chicken breasts.
7. Cover the slow cooker and cook on high for 3–4 hours.
8. Take the breasts out and place them into a clean bowl. Shred the chicken with two forks.
9. Place the shredded chicken back into the slow cooker and let it cook for about 15 more minutes so it can reabsorb all the juice and flavor.
10. You can serve the shredded chicken on buns (with or without coleslaw), over some rice, in salads or wraps, or eat it just the way it is. Either way will be a delicious treat fit for lunch, dinner, or a gathering. Enjoy!

KANSAS CITY-STYLE

THE BEST BBQ CHICKEN DRUMSTICKS

SERVES 7+

PREP TIME: 45 MINUTES | COOK TIME: 45 MINUTES
BRIANNE GRAJKOWSKI | SAN DIEGO, CALIFORNIA

I have the Best BBQ Chicken Drumsticks recipe for you! My husband, Mark, started making barbecue chicken drumsticks years ago and it has been a family favorite ever since. We have perfected the recipe to only three ingredients. It's a very inexpensive meal option that can feed a group of people. You can typically get about 10–15 drumsticks in a pack for about $5–$10. We often cook this dish with a few side dishes when we get together with our whole family or a few friends. It also saves well for leftovers for the week. Bonus!

INGREDIENTS

- 10–15 chicken drumsticks
- 3 tablespoons carne asada seasoning (I used El Mexicano Carne Asada Seasoning)
- 6 ounces barbecue sauce (I used ½ bottle of Sweet Baby Rays Original BBQ Sauce)

DIRECTIONS

1. Start the barbecue.
2. Sprinkle a light even coating of carne asada seasoning on all sides of the drumsticks.
3. Grill for about 45 minutes to 1 hour depending on the thickness of the chicken. Make sure to rotate the chicken a quarter turn every 10–15 minutes to cook all sides evenly.
4. Pour barbecue sauce in a large bowl.
5. Use tongs to coat each piece of chicken evenly with the barbecue sauce.
6. Place each piece on a cookie sheet or serving tray then enjoy!

Gas Grills

It may not offer the most fragrant, smoky flavor one often desires, but gas/propane grills are a more controllable and time-saving alternative. And now, many grills offer wood chip holders that can give you that great smoky flavor.

TEXAS-
STYLE

Here we are; we made it to Texas. In this region, there are several kinds of barbecue styles, but the two regions we'll focus on the most are Central and Eastern Texas. Central Texas barbecue, known for its oak-smoked brisket served without sauce, is best described as "what you think of" when it comes to Texas barbecue. Beef is simply seasoned with salt and pepper, then smoked low and slow. The meat is the star, and the sauce and sides are an afterthought, if offered at all. Eastern Texas-style includes both beef and pork, often served as a sandwich with a spicy, vinegar-based sauce that soaks into buttery buns, and plenty of sides.

CENTRAL TEXAS

AUTHENTIC CENTRAL TEXAS BRISKET

BEEF SHORT RIBS "DINO BONES"

COWBOY BREAD BOWL BRISKET STEW

EASY SLOW COOKER BBQ PULLED PORK

HORN BEEF RIBS

ROSA'S RIBS

SMOKED BABY BACKS WITH CHERRY CHIPOTLE GLAZE

SMOKED PORK BELLY TACOS WITH POBLANO SAUCE

STRAWBERRY SODA PORK SPARERIBS

EASTERN TEXAS

BBQ PORK RIBS WITH MUSTARD BOURBON SAUCE

PORK BELLY BURNT ENDS

SWEET BBQ RIBS

AUTHENTIC CENTRAL TEXAS BRISKET

SERVES 7+

PREP TIME: 45 MINUTES | COOK TIME: 6+ HOURS

SEAN MILLER | SPANISH FORT, ALABAMA

I made my first Central Texas-style brisket in early 2016. I watched some YouTube videos about Central Texas brisket from various pitmasters and did my best effort, and kept at it through trial and error. My wife is from Texas, so as she started to say it was legitimate, I then had countless other Texans tell me that my brisket was incredible and even got requests for more! I live in Southern Alabama near the Gulf Coast, but in the summer of 2022, I visited Lockhart, Texas (barbecue capital of Texas) and visited legendary Central Texas barbecue restaurants. I confirmed once and for all that my brisket recipe and process produced an authentic result.

Brisket is the king of true barbecue, and especially Central Texas barbecue. People often shy away from making brisket, as it can be a challenge due a variety of factors. Each brisket is unique depending on the individual cow, how it was raised, what the cow ate, and even how long it has been in the vacuum-seal bag after butchering. However, with a few key steps, you will be on your way to eating incredibly delicious brisket that will leave your family and friends craving more!

INGREDIENTS

- 1 whole USDA prime brisket (12–16 pounds)
- ¼ cup kosher salt
- ¼ cup 16-mesh coarse black pepper
- ¼ cup avocado or olive oil for the binder

DIRECTIONS

1. Start the smoker and maintain heat at an average of 250°F. Depending on your smoker, place a water pan either underneath where the brisket will go, or between the firebox and where the brisket will be.

2. Trim the brisket by first slicing or removing anything that's loose on either side from the butchering process, as well as anything discolored. Next, take the fat cap down to about ¼-inch thickness all around. Remove the two hard sections of fat on the point, the larger known as the "deckle." Remove any super thin sections of the flat by cutting a straight line on each long side of the brisket rectangle. Lastly, round the edges on the flat.

3. Season the brisket! Rub oil on the brisket as a binder for the seasoning. Then, take your rub and season generously. Flip the brisket over and repeat the process, this time getting rub on the sides. A ½ cup of rub should be sufficient for an average 12–16-pound brisket, but you can always add/subtract if desired.

4. Then, smoke. For the first 4 hours, don't open the lid, don't put in a leave-in thermometer probe, don't check on it, don't do anything. Just simply smoke the brisket at an average of 225°F–250°F. If using a traditional off-set smoker, be sure to have a clear, wispy smoke with a blueish tint. Billowy smoke is dirty smoke.

5. After 4 hours, check on the brisket and spritz with your choice of liquid. I personally use water, but you can use apple cider vinegar, water and apple juice, water and bourbon, the sky is the limit. The key is keeping it moist. Check the brisket every hour (after the original 4 hours of not touching it) to make sure edges and such aren't drying out.

6. Insert a leave-in thermometer if desired, preferably around the middle of the brisket. Note: There will be a "stall" around the 150°F–165°F internal temperature mark; this means that the temperature will not rise even by 1° for a very long time. This is okay! Keep smoking at 250°F and don't panic. This is the process where the brisket will reduce in size and the rendering process is cooling off the brisket.

7. When the internal temperature of brisket is around 170°F, the "bark" should look good enough to eat. Wrap it in unwaxed butcher paper. Take two long sheets (about 3 feet or more) of butcher paper and place them overlapping each other. Take your spray bottle

and generously spray the butcher paper. Place the brisket on the paper, spray the top of the brisket generously, and then fold tightly two times, tucking the remaining paper underneath the brisket.

8. Place the wrapped brisket into a full-size aluminum pan and place back into the smoker. Run the smoker hotter at 250°F–265°F to finish.

9. Start checking the brisket around the 198°F–203°F internal temperature mark. It must be "probe tender," meaning that there is zero resistance when a thermometer probe is inserted in the flat of the brisket.

10. Let it rest to allow the juices to be reabsorbed into the muscle fibers. It is absolutely vital to let the still-wrapped brisket in the aluminum pan sit out on the kitchen counter, uncovered, for at least 30 minutes to give off the carry over heat. If you will be eating this brisket in the next 3–4 hours, cover the wrapped brisket in the pan with aluminum foil and put it in the bottom of a cooler. Place 4–5 old towels on top and close your cooler. It will stay very hot and food safe for 3–4 hours. If you need to hold the brisket longer than 3–4 hours, then after 4 hours in the cooler, switch to your kitchen oven at 170°F (or 150°F if your oven is capable).

11. Serve after your brisket has sufficiently rested (1–2 hours minimum). Unwrap the brisket while still inside the aluminum pan to capture any remaining juices in the pan. Take the brisket and slice ¼-inch slices of the flat against the grain. When you get about halfway down to the point section, flip the brisket 90° and slice the point section in thicker slices, about ½-inch slices. Pour the pan juices over your slices and enjoy all your hard work with family and friends!

HOT TIP

Butcher paper will help the brisket to breathe better as it finishes cooking. You can also use foil, but I personally don't recommend that, as it can soften the bark too much and if you don't watch it very carefully, you will end up with smoked pot roast from the braising that happens in foil.

BEEF SHORT RIBS "DINO BONES"

SERVES 4

PREP TIME: 30 MINUTES | COOK TIME: 6+ HOURS

SEAN MILLER | SPANISH FORT, ALABAMA

To me, smoked beef short ribs are the quintessential barbecue experience. Decadent in both flavor and presentation, properly made "dino bones" create core barbecue memories for whoever gets the chance to eat them. Beef short ribs are essentially "brisket on a stick," as plate short ribs are basically brisket point in location on the cow. However, it's important to note that not all short ribs are the same. Most of the time, grocery store short ribs are going to be taken from the chuck, and if you ask the butcher behind the counter for short ribs, check the amount of bones. If there are four rib bones in the package, then those are chuck short ribs. If there are three rib bones, then they are plate short ribs. The plate short ribs are going to give you that decadent brisket experience. Chuck short ribs are still going to be delicious, and this recipe can still be followed, but they are different in taste, size, and juiciness.

True, genuine Central Texas barbecue is simply 50/50 kosher salt and 16-mesh coarse black pepper. That's it. However, I personally encourage you to experiment with adding espresso-grind coffee to the mix, including simply taking your favorite barbecue rub and using equal parts of espresso-grind coffee, barbecue rub, kosher salt, and 16-mesh coarse black pepper. However, barbecue purists will tell you simply 50/50 salt and pepper is the way to be for Central Texas barbecue!

INGREDIENTS

- 1 rack of plate short ribs
- ⅛ cup 16-mesh coarse black pepper
- ⅛ cup kosher salt
- Avocado or olive oil for the binder
- Spray bottle of water

DIRECTIONS

1. Start the smoker and maintain heat at an average of 265°F. Depending on your smoker, place a water pan either underneath where the beef ribs will go, or place the water pan in between the firebox and where the beef ribs will be.

2. Trim the beef ribs. There is usually both a thick top layer of fat and a thick silver skin that must be removed. When you finish trimming the short ribs, you should see marbled beef as the majority. Some of the fat can stay, but all silver skin must be removed. Don't worry about the tough membrane on the bottom, as the membrane keeps it all together when slicing at the end.

3. Season the beef ribs by rubbing your oil of choice on the beef ribs as a binder for the seasoning. Then, take your rub and generously season the top and sides of your beef ribs. Don't worry about seasoning the bottom, as that tough membrane isn't consumed.

4. Smoke the ribs! Beef short ribs are the easiest cut of barbecue to cook. They almost "self-baste" in their own rendered fat due to the very high marbling, so you almost don't even have to spritz them as you would brisket or other smoked meat. Simply keep an eye on them, and if edges start to look dry, spritz them as needed with water or the liquid of your choice. You also don't have to worry about changing the temperature or wrapping them. They just simply smoke at around 265°F until done. That's it! For an average rack of short ribs, you are looking at around 8–10 hours or so.

5. Finish the ribs. You also don't have to worry about overcooking beef ribs, but you do need to worry about undercooking them. Make sure to fully render the fat so each bite is almost fork tender. This will be achieved around the 205°F internal mark, but don't go by temperature. Like with brisket, beef short ribs are done when it is "probe tender." This means it feels like a thermometer probe going through room temp butter. Once there's zero resistance in the beef ribs to the thermometer probe, they are done and can be taken off the smoker to rest.

6. Let the ribs rest. An essential step in the process, they should rest for a minimum of 30 minutes before carving to allow the juices to redistribute back into the meat. You can rest them for longer using the steps described in my brisket recipe.

7. Serve! Simply slice the beef ribs in between the bones and enjoy the best bite in barbecue! They should be "bite tender" when properly done, meaning you can easily eat them right off the bone.

COWBOY BREAD BOWL BRISKET STEW

MAKES 2 BOWLS

PREP TIME: 1 HOUR | COOK TIME: 5 HOURS

TROY CAMP | BREA, CALIFORNIA

This a recipe we've been making for many years. When you do competition barbecue, you end up with tons of leftover meats and this is a great way to use leftover brisket!

INGREDIENTS

BRISKET:
- One 1-pound brisket
- Brisket rub of your choice, to season
- 10 ounces beef consommé
- 1 cup water

BREAD BOWL BRISKET STEW:
- 1 white onion, chopped
- ½ stick butter, melted
- 3 tablespoons flour
- 1 tablespoon chopped garlic
- 1½ pounds small red skin potatoes, diced
- 1 pound baby carrots, diced
- 3 stalks of celery, sliced
- One 14½-ounce can diced tomatoes
- One 4-ounce can diced green chiles
- 2 round cuts sourdough bread, hollowed out

DIRECTIONS

BRISKET:
1. Rub the brisket with the brisket rub.
2. Heat smoker to 325°F.
3. Add the brisket to the smoker, fat side down. Smoke for 45 minutes.
4. Flip the brisket and smoke for 2 hours.
5. Place the meat in aluminum pan, fat side down. Pour the beef consommé and water into the pan. Cover with foil.
6. Return to the smoker for about 2 hours or until the internal temperature is about 210°F.
7. Let rest 1 hour before slicing into cubes.

BREAD BOWL BRISKET STEW:
1. When ready, cube the brisket into bite-sized portions.
2. Add the cubed brisket to a Dutch oven or slow cooker.
3. Add the chopped onion and cook a few minutes.
4. Add the melted butter and flour and stir until the mixture starts to thicken.
5. Add the garlic and vegetables and mix well.
6. Let cook for 1 hour or until carrots and potatoes are tender (stir occasionally).
7. Divide between two bread bowls, or serve with rolls or biscuits.

EASY SLOW COOKER BBQ PULLED PORK

SERVES 4

PREP TIME: 30 MINUTES | COOK TIME: 6+ HOURS
SARA LUNDBERG | PORTLAND, OREGON

I owe this delightful recipe to my awesome coworker. It never fails to please a crowd, and the best part is how incredibly simple it is to prepare. It's pure happiness on a plate!

INGREDIENTS

TEXAS BARBECUE SAUCE:

- 1 tablespoon butter
- 2 garlic cloves, minced
- 1 cup ketchup
- ¼ cup dark brown sugar, packed
- ⅓ cup lemon juice
- 3 tablespoons apple cider vinegar
- 1 tablespoon yellow mustard
- 2 tablespoons tomato paste
- 2 teaspoons chili powder
- 1 tablespoon Worcestershire sauce

BARBECUE PULLED PORK:

- 2 tablespoons extra virgin olive oil
- One 5–6-pound boneless pork shoulder roast
- 2 teaspoons garlic powder
- 2 teaspoons dried onion flakes
- 2 teaspoons oregano
- 2 teaspoons salt
- 2 teaspoons pepper
- 1 large onion, cut into ½-inch slices

DIRECTIONS

TEXAS BARBECUE SAUCE:

1. In a generously sized saucepan, melt the butter over medium heat.
2. Add the garlic and cook for an additional minute.
3. Stir in the rest of the ingredients and bring the mixture to a gentle boil.
4. Reduce the heat and let it simmer, uncovered, for about 15–20 minutes, allowing the flavors to beautifully meld together.

BARBECUE PULLED PORK:

1. To begin, heat the oil in a cast iron skillet on high heat for approximately 5 minutes.
2. In a large bowl, generously coat the pork with the garlic, onion flakes, oregano, salt, and pepper on all sides.
3. Transfer the seasoned pork to the skillet and sear it over medium-high heat, ensuring each side turns a delicious brown (around 15 minutes).
4. In the slow cooker, arrange the onion slices on the bottom and place the seared pork on top.
5. Pour in 1–2 cups of the Texas Barbecue Sauce (recipe above), depending on taste.
6. Cook on high for 4 hours or on low for 8 hours.
7. Finally, shred the tender pork with forks and add the remaining barbecue sauce. Enjoy!

HORN BEEF RIBS

SERVES 2

PREP TIME: 15 MINUTES | COOK TIME: 7 HOURS

MATT HORN | OAKLAND, CALIFORNIA

This recipe was developed at my restaurant, Horn Barbecue. Through trial and error, we came up with a recipe that uses five simple ingredients to create succulent, perfectly seasoned beef with a satisfying smoky finish.

INGREDIENTS

- 2 racks beef ribs (about 4–6 ribs per rack)
- ¼ cup kosher salt
- ¼ cup cracked black pepper
- ¼ cup smoked paprika
- 2 tablespoons onion powder
- 2 tablespoons garlic powder
- 2 teaspoons dried mustard
- 1 teaspoon cayenne pepper (optional, for heat)
- Your choice of wood chunks or logs (oak, hickory, or pecan work great with beef)

HOT TIP

If your ribs start to look too dark or dry during the smoke, you can wrap them in butcher paper or aluminum foil with a splash of beef broth. This is often referred to as the "Texas Crutch" and can help the ribs retain moisture.

Remember, the key to successful low and slow barbecue is patience. It's ready when it's ready. Monitor the smoker's temperature closely, adjust vents as necessary, and keep the smoke clean (avoid thick, white smoke).

Serve with your favorite barbecue sauce on the side, though these ribs will have a ton of flavor on their own!

DIRECTIONS

PREPARATION:

1. Mix all the dry ingredients together in a bowl to make your rub.
2. Clean the ribs, removing the membrane from the back if it's still attached. This will allow the rub to better penetrate the meat and will improve the texture of the final product.
3. Generously apply the rub on both sides of the beef ribs. For best results, let them marinate for at least 2 hours, or overnight in the refrigerator.

SET UP YOUR SMOKER:

1. Prepare your offset wood-burning smoker by cleaning out any old ashes.
2. Start a small fire in the offset chamber using charcoal. Once the charcoal is glowing red and covered with gray ash, add a couple of wood chunks or logs.
3. Adjust the vents to establish a stable temperature of around 225°F to 250°F. You'll need to monitor the temperature and add wood as needed throughout the smoking process.

SMOKE THE RIBS:

1. Once the smoker is at the desired temperature, place the beef ribs bone side down in the main chamber, away from the firebox.
2. Maintain the smoker's temperature, adding more wood chunks or logs as needed. You'll also want to rotate the ribs every couple of hours to ensure even cooking.
3. If you have a meat thermometer, you're aiming to slowly bring the internal temperature of the ribs to about 200°F. This could take around 7 to 8 hours, but trust the texture and appearance more than the clock. The ribs should have a dark crust (or bark) and be tender enough to tear apart with your hands.

REST AND SERVE:

1. Once done, remove the ribs from the smoker and let them rest for about 20–30 minutes. This allows the juices to redistribute throughout the meat.
2. Slice between the bones, serve, and enjoy!

ROSA'S RIBS

SERVES 3

PREP TIME: 1 HOUR, 30 MINUTES | COOK TIME: 5 HOURS
DANTE BATTEN | SCRANTON, PENNSYLVANIA

This recipe was passed down from my grandmother, Rosa Dorsey. She was neighbors and best friends with Rosa Parks in Montgomery, Alabama. During this time, my grandmother created meals and barbecue for African Americans who weren't able to attend local restaurants because of racial tensions. Rosa's Ribs was a hit when our first restaurant launched in 2016, and we even won Business of the Year from the University of Scranton. It's an easy recipe that will satisfy the taste of any guest.

INGREDIENTS

- 1 rack of St. Louis-style ribs
- Vinegar, to soak ribs

ROSA'S DRY RUB:
- ¼ cup pink Himalayan salt
- ¼ cup ground black pepper
- 2 tablespoons smoked paprika
- 2 tablespoons chili powder
- 2 tablespoons garlic powder
- 2 tablespoons onion powder
- 1 tablespoon thyme

ROSA'S BARBECUE SAUCE:
- ¼ cup tomato paste
- ½ cup dark soy sauce
- 1 cup raw honey
- 2 tablespoons lime juice
- 1 cup light brown sugar
- 2 tablespoons liquid smoke
- 1 tablespoon ground ginger

DIRECTIONS

1. Soak St. Louis-style ribs in vinegar for 20 minutes.
2. Rinse and pat dry.
3. Make the Rosa's Dry Rub by mixing the salt, pepper, paprika, chili powder, garlic powder, onion powder, and thyme together in a bowl.
4. Evenly distribute the rub through the entire rack of ribs. You can use a tablespoon of oil to help spread the seasoning.
5. Tightly wrap the ribs with aluminum foil on both sides.
6. Smoke the ribs for 4 hours at 365°F.
7. Make the Rosa's Barbecue Sauce by mixing tomato paste, soy sauce, honey, lime juice, brown sugar, liquid smoke, and ginger together in a bowl. Let sit for 1 hour.

SMOKED BABY BACKS
WITH CHERRY CHIPOTLE GLAZE

SERVES 4

PREP TIME: 15 MINUTES | COOK TIME: 5 HOURS, 15 MINUTES
2CHEFS | AUSTIN TEXAS

Living in Austin, Texas, we are surrounded by some of the best barbecue in the world. So, when we're cooking for our private chef clients, we choose to keep our barbecue recipes fairly simple, letting the meat speak for itself, then we pair it with seasonal ingredients to send it over the top. This glaze will blow minds with the tart cherries, spicy chipotle peppers, and that smoky flavor we all love!

INGREDIENTS

RIBS:
- 4 pounds baby back pork ribs
- 2 tablespoons brown sugar
- 1 tablespoon sea salt
- 1 tablespoon coarse black pepper
- 1 tablespoon onion powder
- 1 tablespoon garlic powder
- 1 tablespoon seafood seasoning (We used Old Bay)
- 1 tablespoon smoked paprika

CHERRY CHIPOTLE GLAZE:
- 10 ounces pitted red cherries (fresh or frozen)
- 2 chipotle peppers
- 1 tablespoon balsamic vinegar
- 1 tablespoon honey
- 1 tablespoon brown sugar
- ½ teaspoon salt

DIRECTIONS

1. Preheat your smoker to 180°F with the lid closed for at least 15 minutes.

2. Prepare your ribs by removing the silver skin membrane from the bone side of the ribs by working the tip of a knife underneath the membrane. Use paper towels to get a firm grip, then rip the membrane off.

3. In a small bowl, combine all the spices and brown sugar, then sprinkle the mixture evenly on all sides of the ribs.

4. Place the ribs in the preheated smoker and smoke them meat side up for 3 hours.

5. While the ribs are smoking, make the glaze. Place all of the glaze ingredients into a blender and blend until smooth. Place the mixture in a saucepan over medium-low heat and simmer for 25 minutes, or until it looks thick and jam-like. Remove from heat and let cool to room temperature.

6. Once the ribs have smoked for 3 hours, remove the ribs and increase the temperature to 225°F. Apply some of the Cherry Chipotle Glaze evenly with a brush, fully covering the ribs, and then wrap them completely in aluminum foil. Return the foiled ribs to the grill and cook for an additional 2 hours.

7. Carefully remove the ribs from the foil, apply another even layer of the glaze, and allow to rest for 10–15 minutes before serving.

SMOKED PORK BELLY TACOS

SERVES 7+

WITH POBLANO SAUCE

PREP TIME: 30 MINUTES | COOK TIME: 6+ HOURS

MARCUS RUIZ | HOUSTON, TEXAS

I know Texas is normally known for beef, but growing up in my family, it was always pork that we had for our Sunday family dinners. When I found out about this opportunity, I wanted to create a recipe that my family would enjoy, so I actually worked on this on a Sunday and was able to feed my family lunch because of it. Culturally speaking, tacos are huge in Texas. There's nothing better than wrapping up some perfectly smoked meat in a corn or flour tortilla and hitting it with some onion, cilantro, and salsa. So while this recipe itself wasn't passed down from a family member, it was definitely inspired by my family.

INGREDIENTS

PORK BELLY:
- 2–3 pounds pork belly
- 4 tablespoons yellow mustard

SEASONING:
- ¼ cup coarse black pepper
- ¼ cup coarse salt
- ⅛ cup granulated garlic
- ⅛ cup garlic powder

GARLIC CONFIT:
- 1 bulb garlic
- 2 tablespoons oil of choice
- Sprinkle of above seasoning

POBLANO CREMA:
- 2 poblano peppers
- 1 bunch cilantro
- 8 ounces Mexican crema
  (I used Nestle Media Crema Table Cream)

TACOS:
- Tortillas, flour or corn
- 5–6 radishes, sliced
- Freshly chopped cilantro

DIRECTIONS

SEASONING:
1. Add the black pepper, salt, garlic powder, and granulated garlic in a bowl or shaker and mix well.

PORK BELLY:
1. Heat the smoker up to 225°F.
2. Pat the pork belly dry with paper towels or napkins.
3. Score the fat cap (the side that is all white from the fat) in a crosshatch pattern. Note: You're only looking to cut about ¼ of an inch into it. You only want to cut into the fat, not the entire pork belly.
4. Lather one side with the yellow mustard and then generously season.
5. Repeat on the other side and be sure to season the sides.
6. Let it sit at room temperature for about 20 minutes and let it sweat.
7. Once your smoker is up to temperature, place the meat on and let it smoke.
8. This is a no wrap cook, so just let your meat sit on the pit until it hits about 200°F internal temperature. Depending on how much your pork belly weighs, it could take anywhere from 6–8 hours.
9. Once it's finished, let it rest for at least 30 minutes and then cut it into 1-inch x 1-inch cubes.

GARLIC CONFIT (KIND OF):
1. Find the top of the garlic bulb and cut off enough of it to expose each individual piece of garlic. You will cut off some of the actual garlic pieces themselves and that's what you want.
2. Place the cut garlic in aluminum foil and add 2 tablespoons of your oil of choice, along with some seasoning.
3. Add the garlic to the smoker and let it cook for an hour or until it's softened.

POBLANO CREMA:

1. Roast the poblanos directly over a flame. An open fire or a gas stove can work great for this.

2. Once the peppers are blackened on all sides, place in a plastic or resealable bag to sweat.

3. After about 10–15 minutes, pull the peppers out of the bag and peel off as much of the outer skin as you can.

4. Cut off the tops of the peppers and add them to a blender.

5. Add the crema and cilantro (the entire bunch), and squeeze the garlic into the blender as well. Add salt and pepper to taste.

6. Blend until it is nice and smooth.

Scan QR Code to watch.

STRAWBERRY SODA PORK SPARERIBS

SERVES 3

PREP TIME: 1 HOUR, 30 MINUTES | COOK TIME: 4 HOURS, 30 MINUTES

KELLI NEVAREZ | PALACIOS, TEXAS

This is sweet rib recipe that has always been a family favorite at any potluck we've had at my parents' home. A strawberry cream soda was incorporated into our rib recipe, which is scaled to feed the masses of aunts, uncles, cousins, and friends. Any strawberry soda can be used. (We use Big Red soda, which is a Texas barbecue staple.)

INGREDIENTS

PORK SPARERIBS:
- One 3–4-pound rack of St. Louis pork spareribs
- 32 ounces strawberry soda
- ¼ cup dry pork rub (your choice)
- 2 cups Strawberry Soda Barbecue Sauce (ingredients below)
- 1 sheet heavy aluminum foil

STRAWBERRY SODA BARBECUE SAUCE:
- 4 cups strawberry soda
- 2 cups ketchup
- 1 cup strawberry preserves
- ¾ cup brown sugar
- ¼ cup apple cider vinegar
- 2 tablespoons molasses
- 1 tablespoon dry mustard
- 1 teaspoon paprika
- 1 teaspoon kosher salt
- 1 teaspoon black pepper (restaurant grind)

DIRECTIONS

STRAWBERRY SODA BARBECUE SAUCE:
1. Blend all of the ingredients until the mixture is smooth. Pour the sauce into a pot and simmer to combine the flavors while the sauce is thickened. Remove from heat and let rest until cool.

PORK SPARERIBS:
1. Trim and prep the ribs by removing the rear flap and trimming any jagged edges. The rear membrane is not removed. This allows the ribs to be cooked to a more tender state without the meat falling off the bone. Any loose edges will burn and dry out. They are trimmed before smoking.
2. Spray the rib rack with the strawberry soda. This acts as a binder for the pork spice.
3. Coat both sides of the rib rack with your favorite dry pork rub.
4. Place your ribs on an offset smoker at 265°F.
5. After an hour, lightly spray the rib rack with soda again.
6. Smoking the ribs for 3 hours total ensures a smoky flavor and great color.
7. After 3 hours, wrap the ribs in heavy aluminum foil. Place the ribs meat side up. The foil seam will also be up to keep the juices from leaking out of the wrapped foil packet.
8. Smoke the ribs to an internal temperature of 185°F. The rack should be limber and fold over while holding it in both hands.
9. Remove the rack from the foil and brush on the Strawberry Soda Barbecue Sauce on the meat side.
10. Place the rack back in the smoker for 15 minutes or until the sauce sets.
11. Remove rack and let rest a few minutes before serving.
12. Slice the rack between the bones.
13. Save the extra sauce for your guests to enjoy.

Buy High-Quality Meat

There is no factor (preparing, cooking, seasoning, marinating) as important as having high-quality meat. Buying direct from local farmers is best, but butcher shops that source high-quality, fresh, and responsibly raised animals are a great place to shop. Remember: any butcher should be able to tell you exactly where their meat came from and how it was fed/raised.

BBQ PORK RIBS

SERVES 4

WITH MUSTARD BOURBON SAUCE

PREP TIME: 1 HOUR, MARINATE OVERNIGHT | COOK TIME: 1 HOUR

There's nothing quite like a plate of classic barbecue pork ribs, but what makes this recipe stand out is the mustard bourbon sauce. Tangy, zesty, and delicious, these ribs will surely become a go-to favorite.

INGREDIENTS

MUSTARD BOURBON BARBECUE SAUCE:

- 1 teaspoon vegetable oil
- 1 bunch scallions, chopped
- 1 medium onion, chopped
- 4 large cloves garlic, chopped
- 7 ounces packed golden brown sugar
- ½ cup ketchup
- ⅓ cup tomato purée
- 4 ounces grainy Dijon mustard
- 4 ounces water
- ⅓ cup Worcestershire sauce
- ⅓ cup apple cider vinegar
- ⅓ cup apple juice
- 1 chipotle chili in adobo sauce, finely chopped
- 1 teaspoon ground cumin
- 1½ cups bourbon

PORK RIBS:
- 3½ pounds baby back pork ribs

DRY RUB:
- 2 tablespoons ground cumin
- 1 tablespoon chili powder
- 1 tablespoon dry mustard powder
- 1 tablespoon coarse sea salt
- 1½ teaspoons cayenne pepper
- 1½ teaspoons ground cardamom
- 1½ teaspoons ground cinnamon

DIRECTIONS

MUSTARD BOURBON BARBECUE SAUCE:

1. Heat the oil in a heavy, large saucepan over medium-low heat.

2. Add the scallions, onion, and garlic and sauté until tender, about 15 minutes. Mix in the remaining ingredients, adding the bourbon last.

3. Simmer the sauce until thick and reduced to 1¼ pints stirring occasionally, about 1 hour.

4. Season to taste with salt and pepper. This sauce can be prepared two weeks ahead.

5. Cover and refrigerate.

PORK RIBS AND DRY RUB:

1. Mix the ingredients for the dry rub in a medium bowl. Rub the mixture over both sides of the rib racks. Arrange the ribs on a large baking sheet. Cover and refrigerate overnight.

2. Preheat the barbecue to medium. Cut the rib racks into 4- to 6-rib sections. Arrange the ribs on the barbecue. Grill until the meat is tender, occasionally turning the ribs with tongs, about 40 minutes. Using tongs, transfer the ribs to a work surface.

3. Cut the rib sections between the bones into individual ribs. Arrange on a clean baking sheet. Brush the ribs with half of the Mustard Bourbon Barbecue Sauce. Place the remaining sauce in a small saucepan and reserve.

4. Return the ribs to the barbecue. Place the pan of reserved sauce at the edge of the barbecue to reheat. Grill the ribs until brown and crisp on the edges, brushing with more sauce and turning occasionally, about 10 minutes. Serve the ribs with warm sauce.

PORK BELLY BURNT ENDS

SERVES 7+

PREP TIME: 30 MINUTES | COOK TIME: 5 HOURS, 30 MINUTES

SEAN MILLER | SPANISH FORT, ALABAMA

I love bacon, and I love barbecue, so when I first found out about pork belly burnt ends, I knew I had to make them! I've experimented with different ways of making them over the years, and this has repeatably been one of the best dishes to bring to a party! Pork Belly Burnt Ends have quickly become one of the most popular bites in barbecue. A pork-take on the ever-popular brisket burnt ends of Kansas City, it combines everything you love about bacon and barbecue and brings them together!

INGREDIENTS

- 8–10 pounds skinless pork belly
- ½ cup your favorite barbecue seasoning
- One bottle your favorite barbecue sauce (make sure it's a thick/sticky sauce)
- Spray bottle of water or preferred liquid

HOT TIP

Not all of the fat renders while cooking, so your resulting bite could be very fatty if the fat/meat ratio is too high. For example, for cuts with a lot of fat, like those that are 75% fat, you can trim some of that fat off before cooking.

DIRECTIONS

1. Start up your smoker and seek to smoke at an average of 250°F–265°F. Place a water pan in your smoker to add moisture to the chamber, as well as be a shield between the heat and the pork belly.

2. Cut the pork belly into 2-inch cubes. Investigate each cube, and if there is significant fat, trim as desired.

3. Season the pork belly cubes liberally with your favorite barbecue seasoning. It will be covered in a sweet sauce later in the cook, so don't be afraid to over-season, as you need the seasoning to cut through the sweet sauce to balance it all out.

4. Place the pork belly cubes on your smoker and spritz every hour with a liquid of your choice (I personally spray with just water).

5. After 3 hours on the smoker, the pork belly burnt ends should have bark formed and should have reduced in size. If not, continue smoking them for an additional hour.

6. Place the pork belly cubes into a half-sized aluminum pan and toss in your favorite barbecue sauce. You can also add honey or a hot honey, as well as adding bourbon and/or brown sugar if desired. The sky is the limit! I would NOT recommend adding butter, as there is sufficient fat in pork belly already.

7. Cover the pan with foil and place back in the smoker for 2 more hours at 275°F average. Do not remove foil during these two hours.

8. Remove foil, toss pork belly cubes with a set of tongs, drain some of the sauce if desired, and place back in the smoker uncovered for 30 minutes at 275°F. This will help "set" the sauce on the pork belly burnt ends.

9. Serve and enjoy! You should have a fork-tender pork belly bite that is sweet, salty, and delicious!

SWEET BBQ RIBS

SERVES 6

PREP TIME: 2 HOURS | COOK TIME: 45 MINUTES

Make your ribs savory-sweet with this recipe that incorporates pineapple juice and honey. You can also add a touch of spice by adding pepper shavings on top for a subtle kick!

Prime, Choice, or Select. What's Your Beef?

Prime: Some to significant marbling. Prime roasts and steaks are excellent for grilling.

Choice: High-quality but less marbling than prime. Choice steaks and roasts are tender, juicy, and flavorful. Great for dry-heat cooking.

Select: Leaner than the higher grades. Fairly tender, but it may lack juiciness because it has less marbling. Cook with dry heat only with the tender cuts.

INGREDIENTS

- 3 small pork racks, cut into single ribs
- 1 tablespoon olive oil
- 4 cloves garlic, peeled and crushed
- ½ cup tomato purée
- ½ cup pineapple juice
- ½ cup balsamic vinegar
- ¼ cup soy sauce
- ¾ cup honey
- Sea salt and freshly ground black pepper

DIRECTIONS

1. Place the ribs in a shallow pan. Combine all of the remaining ingredients and pour over the ribs to coat. Transfer the pan to the fridge and marinate for 2 hours.

2. Remove the ribs from the marinade, brushing off any excess. Retain the marinade.

3. Barbecue the ribs over medium heat for 20–30 minutes or until well-browned, cooked, and caramelized on the outside. Place the remaining marinade in a saucepan and reduce by half over a low heat.

4. When the ribs are done, place on a serving plate and pour over the reduced marinade. Serve immediately.

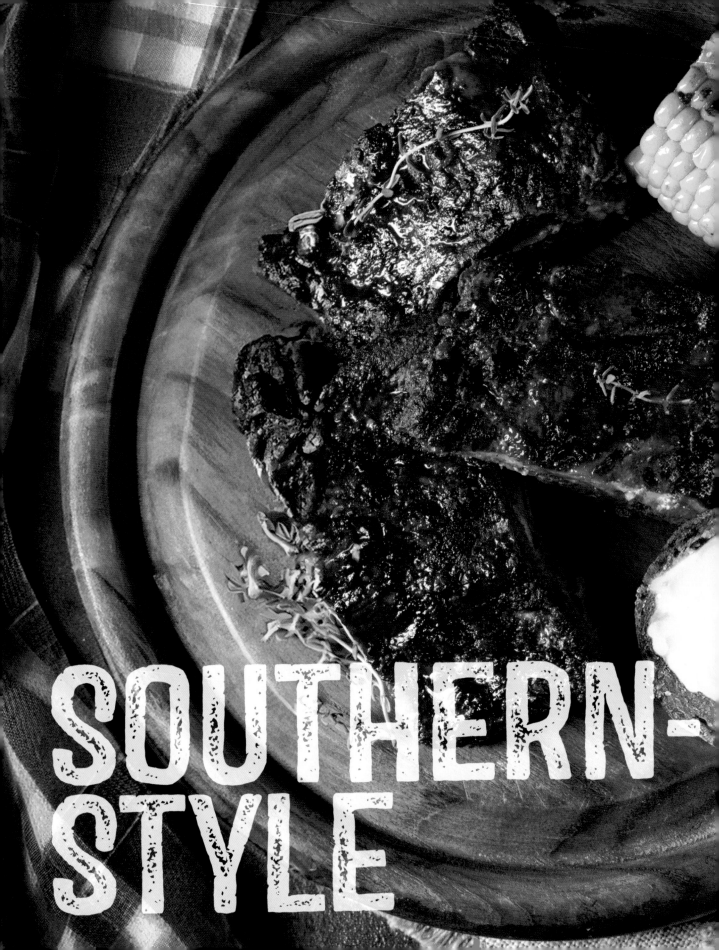

SOUTHERN-STYLE

Now we're in my neck of the woods, being a Georgia boy. The South is notorious for some amazing home cooking, and how they do barbecue is no exception. This section will cover a variety of regional styles, from Memphis—where they're all about pork—to North Carolina—where things get tangy. There's even a Floridian caveman-style recipe, too! Enjoy!

ALABAMA

ROAST CHICKEN WITH ALABAMA WHITE SAUCE, SMASHED POTATOES, AND BACON GREEN BEANS

FLORIDA

CAVEMAN T-BONES WITH HELLFIRE HOT SAUCE

GEORGIA

GEORGIA GOLD CHICKEN

ROAST BELLY OF PORK

KENTUCKY

FALL OFF THE BONE OVEN-BAKED BBQ RIBS

MEMPHIS

CENTRAL CITY BBQ BRISKET CHILI

MEMPHIS BBQ CHICKEN

RENDEZVOUS RIBS

NORTH CAROLINA

APPLE PIE MOONSHINE SPARERIBS

BARBECUED SPARERIBS

SMOKED SPARERIBS

SMOKY COUNTRY-STYLE RIBS (AMISH COMMUNITY COOKBOOK)

TOMATILLOS, JALAPEÑO, AND MEZCAL CAROLINA BBQ STREET TACOS

 Recipes with this symbol represent a gluten-free dish.

ROAST CHICKEN

SERVES 4

WITH ALABAMA WHITE SAUCE, SMASHED POTATOES, AND BACON GREEN BEANS

COOK TIME: 1 HOUR

RYAN PEREL | DALLAS, TEXAS

This is a recipe I created after having Alabama white sauce on a road trip from Kansas City to Chicago. I loved the sauce so much I wanted to pair it with chicken when I got home. I also needed a full meal, so what better than smashed potatoes, which was trending, and bacon green beans.

INGREDIENTS

GLUTEN FREE

- 4 chicken breasts
- Salt, to taste
- Pepper, to taste
- ½ cup mayonnaise
- 2 tablespoons apple cider vinegar
- 2 tablespoons lemon juice
- ½ tablespoon horseradish
- 1 tablespoon mustard
- Dash of cayenne pepper
- 1 tablespoon Worcestershire sauce
- 2 tablespoons brown sugar
- 1½ pounds baby potatoes
- 1 pound green beans, trimmed and steamed
- 6 slices gluten-free bacon, cooked and crumbled
- 3 tablespoons butter
- Olive oil, for drizzling

DIRECTIONS

1. Preheat oven to 400°F. Season chicken with salt and pepper and roast for 30 minutes. Let cool a few minutes, then shred.

2. Combine mayonnaise, vinegar, lemon juice, horseradish, mustard, cayenne, Worcestershire sauce, brown sugar, and salt and pepper. Mix and set aside.

3. Boil potatoes until tender. Drain. Toss in olive oil, salt, and pepper. Smash the potatoes with a spatula and place on a cookie sheet. Drizzle with olive oil and season with salt and pepper. Bake at 425°F for 25 minutes until crispy.

4. Toss cooked green beans in bacon, butter, and salt and pepper.

5. Drizzle sauce over chicken and serve with potatoes and green beans.

HOT TIP

Alabama's distinction is their sauce: a thick, white barbecue sauce made from mayonnaise, vinegar, salt, and pepper.

ALABAMA

CAVEMAN T-BONES

WITH HELLFIRE HOT SAUCE

PREP TIME: 30 MINUTES | COOK TIME: 15 MINUTES

STEVEN RAICHLEN | MIAMI, FLORIDA

The ultimate primal grilling—T-bone steaks charred directly on the embers and topped with an incendiary sauce of jalapeños, cilantro, and garlic. To get the full effect, you must cook the steaks on a bed of charcoal or wood embers. No, you don't need a grill grate. If you don't own a charcoal grill, you can achieve acceptable results by preheating your grill to screaming hot before you put on the steaks. The beauty of this dish is its spontaneity.

Somewhere around 1.8 million years ago, a human ancestor called *Homo Erectus* became the first animal to cook. This recipe pays homage to that first caveman barbecue—with steaks grilled directly on the embers. Of course, the process looks cool as all get out (and I've amazed more than a few people when I've demonstrated Caveman T-bones at *Barbecue University* and on the *Today Show*), but there's a lot more to this dish than mere showmanship. Roasting the steaks on the embers gives the meat a surface charring and smoke flavor you just can't duplicate on a conventional grill. To that, add a sizzling sauce of pan-fried jalapeños, cilantro, and garlic, and you've got T-bones that roar off the plate with flavor that's guaranteed to bring out the caveman in all of us.

INGREDIENTS

STEAKS:
- 4 T-bone steaks (each 12 ounces and 1–1½ inches thick)
- Coarse salt (kosher or sea)
- Cracked black peppercorns

HELLFIRE HOT SAUCE:
- ¾ cup extra virgin olive oil
- 10 jalapeño peppers, thinly sliced crosswise
- 10 cloves garlic, thinly sliced crosswise
- ¾ cup fresh cilantro leaves, coarsely chopped

Note: You'll also need a long-handled cast iron skillet (10 inches in diameter).

DIRECTIONS

1. Build a charcoal fire and rake the coals into an even layer. (Leave the front third of your grill coal free.) When the coals glow orange, fan them with a newspaper or hair dryer to blow off any loose ash.

2. Generously season the steaks on both sides with salt and cracked pepper. Place the steaks directly on the embers about 2 inches apart. Grill until cooked to taste, 3–4 minutes per side for medium-rare, turning with tongs.

3. Using tongs, lift the steaks out of the fire, shaking each to dislodge any embers. Using a basting brush, brush off any loose ash and arrange the steaks on a platter or plates. Let the steaks rest with a sheet of aluminum foil draped over them while you make the sauce. Note: Do not bunch the foil around the steak, or the crust will get soggy.

HELLFIRE HOT SAUCE:

1. Heat the olive oil in a cast-iron skillet directly on the embers. When the oil is hot, add the jalapeños, garlic, and cilantro. Cook over high heat until the chiles and garlic begin to brown, about 2 minutes. Immediately pour over the steaks and serve at once.

GEORGIA GOLD CHICKEN

SERVES 4

PREP TIME: 30 MINUTES | COOK TIME: 30 MINUTES

SARA LUNDBERG | PORTLAND, OREGON

During my time at USC, I had the pleasure of being part of the cooking club, where I created this mouthwatering Georgia Gold Chicken recipe.

INGREDIENTS

- 4 boneless, skinless chicken breasts
- ¼ cup honey
- 2 tablespoons Dijon mustard
- 2 tablespoons soy sauce
- 2 tablespoons olive oil
- 2 cloves garlic, minced
- 1 teaspoon dried thyme
- ½ teaspoon paprika
- Salt and pepper, to taste
- Fresh parsley, for garnish (optional)

DIRECTIONS

1. Preheat oven to 375°F and prepare a baking dish.
2. In a small bowl, whisk together the honey, Dijon mustard, soy sauce, olive oil, garlic, thyme, paprika, salt, and pepper.
3. Place the chicken breasts in the baking dish and pour the marinade on top, making sure the chicken is coated evenly.
4. Let the chicken marinate for at least 30 minutes to allow the flavors to develop.
5. Once marinated, transfer the chicken and the marinade into the preheated oven.
6. Bake for approximately 25–30 minutes or until the chicken is cooked through and reaches an internal temperature of 165°F.
7. While baking, baste the chicken with the marinade every 10 minutes to keep it moist and flavorful.
8. Once cooked, remove the chicken from the oven and let it rest for a few minutes.
9. Serve!

Optional: Garnish with freshly chopped parsley.

GEORGIA

ROAST BELLY OF PORK

SERVES 8

COOK TIME: 2 HOURS, 30 MINUTES
JANE LOVETT | LONDON, ENGLAND

Succulent, melting, slow-roast belly of pork is hard to beat. It's one of the cheapest cuts of meat, which, due to its high fat content and long, slow cooking, remains succulent. This dish also pairs well with a raspberry vinegar; the sweet-sour flavor is the perfect piquant foil to the richness of the pork.

INGREDIENTS

- 5–6 pounds whole pork belly boned and trim, skin very finely scored
- Salt and freshly ground black pepper, to taste
- 1–2 tablespoons all-purpose flour
- Optional: Raspberry vinegar, for serving

HOT TIP

Ask your butcher for a whole pork belly, individually boned. He will take each rib bone out individually, leaving behind as much meat as possible (important as meat is quite scarce on this cut). Secondly, ask him to score the skin very finely, vertically along the joint.

If you can, buy the belly several days before you need it, thus giving the skin time to dry out in the fridge, which in turn produces really crispy crackling.

DIRECTIONS

1. Place the pork in the sink and pour a kettle of boiling water over the skin. Dry on paper towel. This helps to create crispy crackling.

2. Select a roasting tin that's long enough to take the pork comfortably. Using a very large piece of foil, make a rough sausage-shaped mound roughly the same length as the pork. Put this in the roasting tin and gently lie the pork on top. The pork should be sitting on the foil in a rounded arc shape, with no dips and troughs in the skin. Re-mold the foil a little to achieve this if necessary. Moisture will accumulate in any sunken parts during cooking, thus preventing the skin from crackling.

3. Massage a good teaspoon of fine salt into the skin and leave uncovered in the fridge for several days (24 hours minimum). Remove the pork from the fridge for at least an hour before cooking.

4. Preheat the oven 425°F. Rub pork with a little more salt and cook at the top of the hot oven for 20–30 minutes, or until the skin is nicely crackled. Reduce the oven to 325°F and cook slowly for 1½ hours until the pork is meltingly tender. Remove from the tin and leave to rest for at least 20 minutes.

5. To make a slightly thickened gravy, drain any juices from the foil back into the tin. Skim off most of the fat. Remove any odd burnt bits. Stir a tablespoon or so of flour into the fat and juices, then gradually add 1 pint stock or water, stirring all the time to prevent lumps. Bring up to the boil, check the seasoning and pour into a jug. For a thin gravy, omit the flour, scrape off all the goody bits and bubble until syrupy.

Optional: Put some raspberry vinegar on the table in a pretty jug or glass bottle so your guests can pour a little over their pork if desired.

HOT TIP

If the crackling needs crisping up in places at the end of the cooking time (which occasionally it does), give it a burst at the top of a hot oven or under the grill.

FALL OFF THE BONE OVEN-BAKED BBQ RIBS

SERVES 6

PREP TIME: 30 MINUTES | COOK TIME: 3 HOURS

JENNIFER SIKORA | CALVERT CITY, KENTUCKY

I created this recipe during a summer when we were craving ribs, but it was too ungodly hot outside to grill. I learned that going low and slow in the oven can achieve the same low and slow from the grill.

INGREDIENTS

BARBECUE DRY RUB:
- 1½ cups paprika
- ¾ cup brown sugar
- 3¾ tablespoons onion powder

RIBS:
- 2 racks baby back ribs
- 1 cup + extra of your favorite barbecue sauce

DIRECTIONS

1. Mix all the dry rub ingredients together and set them aside.
2. Remove the ribs from the wrapping and wash them off.
3. Remove the silver skin from the back side and pat the ribs dry.
4. Take the dry rub and generously coat the ribs, then wrap them in aluminum foil and place on a sheet pan. Place in the fridge until you are ready to bake.
5. Preheat oven to 300°F. Place the sheet pan in the oven and bake for 3 hours. Remove from the oven and unwrap the ribs.
6. Take your favorite barbecue sauce and baste the front and back of the ribs. Place the ribs back on the sheet pan, then place under the broiler for 5 minutes to caramelize the barbecue sauce on the top of the ribs.

> "BARBECUE MAY NOT BE THE ROAD TO WORLD PEACE, BUT IT'S A START."
> —ANTHONY BORDAIN, CHEF AND TV PERSONALITY

KENTUCKY

CENTRAL CITY BBQ BRISKET CHILI

SERVES 5

PREP TIME: 15 MINUTES | COOK TIME: 30 MINUTES

MARC BONIFACIC | NEW ORLEANS, LOUISIANA

Our Brisket Chili is a big hit at Central City BBQ. When that first cold front hits New Orleans, we know to make some large batches, as the customers put that first of their order. This recipe has been a collaboration of multiple cooks and chefs over the years, and we now feel it's a great addition to our menu.

INGREDIENTS

- 2½ pounds ground brisket
- 1½ cups onion, diced
- 1½ poblano chili, diced
- ¼ cup garlic, minced
- ¼ cup ground cumin
- 2 tablespoons paprika
- ¾ cup dark chili powder
- 1 tablespoon oregano
- ¼ cup kosher salt
- 1 tablespoon coarse black pepper
- 2 quarts water

GARNISH:
- Shredded cheddar cheese
- Sour cream
- Green onion, chopped

DIRECTIONS

1. Cook the ground brisket in a large pan for about 30 minutes over medium heat.

2. Drain the excess fat from the pan. Remove the meat and set aside.

3. Add the onion to the pan and sauté over medium heat for about 3 minutes; then add the poblano pepper and cook for another 2 minutes.

4. Add the brisket back to the pan along with the garlic, water, and other remaining ingredients.

5. Simmer mixture over time to thicken.

6. Serve in a soup cup and garnish with shredded cheddar cheese, sour cream, and green onion. Enjoy!

HOT TIP

If you're in a hurry, a slurry of one tablespoon of cornstarch and a ¼ cup of water can be added to assist with thickening.

MEMPHIS

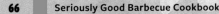

MEMPHIS BBQ CHICKEN

SERVES 4

PREP TIME: 15 MINUTES | COOK TIME: 45 MINUTES
SARA LUNDBERG | PORTLAND, OREGON

Memphis BBQ chicken holds a special place in my heart as a cherished childhood recipe. Cooking it on our backyard grill created incredible memories and flavors. The smoky, tangy sauce perfectly complements the juicy, tender chicken. It's a taste of nostalgia that I'll always cherish.

INGREDIENTS

- 8 bone-in chicken thighs

MEMPHIS BARBECUE SAUCE:

- 1 cup ketchup
- ¼ cup yellow mustard (adjust to taste)
- 2 tablespoons apple cider vinegar
- ¼ cup brown sugar, packed
- 2 tablespoons Worcestershire sauce
- 1 tablespoon chili powder
- 1 teaspoon black pepper
- 1 teaspoon onion powder
- 1 teaspoon garlic powder
- 1 teaspoon celery salt
- 1 teaspoon liquid smoke (optional, but recommended)
- ⅛ to ¼ teaspoon cayenne pepper (adjust to taste)

DIRECTIONS

MEMPHIS BARBECUE SAUCE:

1. In a saucepan, combine the ketchup, yellow mustard, apple cider vinegar, brown sugar, Worcestershire sauce, chili powder, black pepper, onion powder, garlic powder, celery salt, liquid smoke (if desired), and cayenne pepper.
2. Whisk the ingredients together until well blended.
3. Place the mixture in a saucepan over medium heat and bring to a simmer.
4. Reduce the heat to low and let the sauce cook for about 15–20 minutes, stirring occasionally.
5. Taste the sauce and adjust the seasonings according to your preference. Add more mustard or cayenne pepper for extra tang or heat.
6. Once the sauce reaches a desired consistency and flavor, remove it from the heat and let it cool.
7. Transfer the homemade Memphis Barbecue Sauce to a jar or container and refrigerate until ready to use.
8. Enjoy this delightful sauce on grilled chicken, ribs, burgers, or any other barbecue dishes.

MEMPHIS BARBECUE CHICKEN:

1. Preheat barbecue grill to medium-high heat.
2. Season chicken thighs with salt and pepper.
3. Place thighs on grill, skin side down. Cook for 5–7 minutes per side until internal temperature reaches 165°F.
4. Brush Memphis barbecue sauce on both sides of thighs during last few minutes of grilling.
5. Remove from grill and let rest.
6. Serve juicy, saucy barbecue chicken thighs.

RENDEZVOUS RIBS

SERVES 2-4

PREP TIME: 15 MINUTES | COOK TIME: 1 HOUR, 30 MINUTES
ANNA VERGOS BLAIR, IN TRIBUTE TO CHARLIE VERGOS | MEMPHIS, TENNESSE

It all started in 1948. At the time, Charlie Vergos co-owned a meat-and-three restaurant called Wimpy's with his brother-in-law. But they didn't see eye to eye on everything and Charlie decided he'd move into the basement and sell ham sandwiches and beer. There was an old coal chute that he converted into a smoker to give the ham some flavor. He called the place the Rendezvous. By the late 50s, he realized he needed to diversify the menu. After trying his hand at chicken and oysters, his butcher came to him with the one thing he had plenty of: ribs. Ribs had been a staple of backyard barbecues in Memphis neighborhoods for years, but not used in restaurants. So, Vergos came up with the still-used formula: he threw the racks in 18 inches from the fire and grilled them for an hour and 15 minutes to seal in the flavor. A vinegar wash kept them moist, and Vergos created a rub based on the seasoning from his father's unique Greek chili recipe and the Cajun spices he discovered on visits to New Orleans. He added paprika to give it a more traditional barbecue color. And that's it! People went nuts for them. The standard for "Memphis style" barbecue ribs was set over half a century ago in a basement restaurant in downtown Memphis. Come experience it for yourself.

INGREDIENTS

- 2 slabs loin back ribs

RENDEZVOUS BASTE:

- ½ cup water
- ½ cup distilled white vinegar
- ¼ cup barbecue sauce (We used Rendezvous Barbecue Sauce)
- 3 tablespoons barbecue seasoning (We used Rendezvous Famous Seasoning)

DIRECTIONS

1. Grill loin back ribs on a charcoal grill if you've got one.
2. Grill the ribs about 18 inches over charcoal, bone side down first.
3. Prepare the baste and mop over the slabs as they grill.
4. Flip the ribs when they're brown on the underside.
5. Continue basting until there is a nice char on the meat.
6. If you'd like, brush some extra barbecue sauce on top at the end.
7. Sprinkle with more seasoning and enjoy!

Note: It usually takes around 1½ hours, but the best way to tell if they're done is to pick them up on one end and see if they start to separate in the middle.

> "BARBECUE IS THE POETRY OF THE SOUTH.
> IT'S ITS OWN ART FORM."
> —MYRON MIXON, BBQ CHEF, PIT MASTER, AND AUTHOR

MEMPHIS

APPLE PIE MOONSHINE SPARERIBS

SERVES 4

PREP TIME: 1 HOUR, 30 MINUTES | COOK TIME: 4 HOURS, 15 MINUTES
CHRIS GROVE | KNOXVILLE, TENNESSEE

Moonshine is as much a long-time tradition in the South as barbecue. They go together like peas and carrots. It used to be that you had to "know a guy" to get moonshine, but these days, flavored moonshine is found in package stores. If you don't feel like making the barbecue sauce, you can doctor your favorite jarred sauce with the moonshine.

INGREDIENTS

SPARERIBS:
- 1 rack St. Louis-style pork spareribs, trimmed
- 1 ounce high-temperature cooking oil (peanut, canola, etc.)
- ½ cup sweet barbecue rub (I used Flavor Anonymous Notorious RED and Meat Church Honey Hog)
- 1 cup apple juice (divided)
- 6 tablespoons butter, melted
- ¼ cup local honey
- 2 tablespoons brown sugar
- ½ cup Apple Pie Moonshine Barbecue Sauce (see ingredients and recipe)
- ½ teaspoon fine salt
- ¼ teaspoon cayenne

APPLE PIE MOONSHINE BARBECUE SAUCE:
- 1 cup ketchup
- ½ cup brown sugar
- ¾ cup honey
- 3 tablespoons apple cider vinegar
- 1½ tablespoons Worcestershire sauce
- ¼ teaspoon granulated garlic
- ¼ teaspoon onion powder
- 1 teaspoon kosher salt
- ¾ teaspoon chili powder
- ¾ teaspoon black pepper
- ¼ teaspoon cayenne
- ¼ cup apple pie-flavored moonshine

DIRECTIONS

1. Set up and preheat your smoker to 275°F. (We used a Kamado-style grill with a mix of lump charcoal and five to six hickory wood chunks.)

2. Prepare the ribs. Remove the membrane on the back of the ribs. Lightly coat the ribs with the oil. Sprinkle both sides of the ribs with 3 ounces of the rub. Let it rest for about 1 hour.

3. Smoke the ribs. Once the ribs have rested and your smoker is running cleanly at 275°F, place the ribs in the smoker with the meat side facing up. Spritz with apple juice. Let it smoke for 2½ hours, spritzing with apple juice every 45 minutes.

4. Meanwhile, make the sauce. Place all the sauce ingredients in a small pot and bring to a slow simmer. Simmer for 5 minutes, then remove from heat.

5. Wrap the ribs. Place two sheets of foil on top of each other and place the rack of ribs in the center with the meat facing up. Drizzle with half of the honey and butter. Mix the brown sugar and remaining barbecue rub. Sprinkle half of the mixture on the ribs. Flip the ribs to bone side up, repeat the drizzle, and sprinkle. Fold the edges of the foil up and over to form a tight envelope around the ribs.

6. Place the ribs back on the smoker for 90 minutes, meat side down, so the foil seam is facing up. When done, the rack of ribs will be flexible and the tips of the bones will stick out about ½ inch.

7. Glaze the ribs and add a kiss of smoke. Thin ½ cup of the barbecue sauce with about a tablespoon of leftover apple juice. Remove the ribs from the foil pack and glaze them with the sauce. Sprinkle them with the fine salt and cayenne pepper. Place the ribs back on the smoker for 10 minutes to set the sauce and give the ribs one last kiss of smoke.

8. Slice and serve with additional sauce on the side.

NORTH CAROLINA

BARBECUED SPARERIBS

SERVES 5

PREP TIME: 15 MINUTES | COOK TIME: 1 HOUR, 35 MINUTES

Super simple, these spareribs are great for feeding the family as an easy weeknight meal and require everyday ingredients you likely already have stocked in your kitchen. What's more is you can bake them while you take care of whatever else you need to do—two birds, one stone!

INGREDIENTS

- 3 pounds spareribs
- 1 medium onion, chopped
- 1 tablespoon butter
- 1 tablespoon vinegar
- 1 tablespoon sugar
- 2 teaspoons salt
- 3 tablespoons lemon juice
- ½ tablespoon prepared mustard
- ½ cup water
- ½ cup chopped celery
- Dash of pepper
- 1– 2 tablespoons Worcestershire sauce (optional)

DIRECTIONS

1. Wipe ribs with damp cloth and cut into serving size pieces.

2. Place in a shallow baking pan and bake uncovered at 350°F for 30 minutes. Meanwhile, lightly brown onion in butter, then add remaining ingredients. Mix well and simmer 5 minutes.

3. Pour over the spareribs and continue baking for 1 hour longer, basting ribs from time to time with the sauce in the bottom of the pan.

HOT TIP

To clean your barbecue or oven racks, place them on the grass overnight or on a rainy day. The cleanup job is easier!

NORTH CAROLINA

SMOKED SPARERIBS

SERVES 4

PREP TIME: 1 HOUR, 30 MINUTES | COOK TIME: 4 HOURS, 15 MINUTES

MICHAEL LETCHWORTH | AYDEN, NORTH CAROLINA

These ribs are the same preparation and process that we serve at both of our Sam Jones BBQ locations. This recipe is a straightforward, simple way to cook really great ribs without a bunch of steps or ingredients. If you desire more of the fall off the bone style ribs, just cook a little longer in the foil wrap.

INGREDIENTS

- 1 full rack pork spareribs, about 2½ pounds
- 3 ounces your favorite barbecue rub (I used our own Rub Potion)
- 1 gallon brine
- Preferred barbecue sauce, to baste (I used Sam Jones Sweet BBQ Sauce)

DIRECTIONS

1. Brine the meat overnight, then rub it in the morning. The rub can be applied the night before if you're getting started early in the morning, or it can be applied right before you put the slabs on the pit.

2. Evenly coat the ribs with the rub on both sides. Put them bone side down into a 250°F smoker, directly over coals. Let them cook for an hour, then flip and cook for another hour. Check the sag of the rib with a pair of tongs held perpendicular to the rib bones.

3. Once they've reached the proper sag, wrap the ribs in foil and place them back on the 250°F pit for at least another hour. Check for doneness and tenderness. Rewrap and continue cooking if needed.

4. Unwrap them, coat with barbecue sauce, and put back on the pit for 10 minutes longer.

HOT TIP

The wrapping helps to tenderize the ribs, but it also buys you some time. If you're at home executing an entire meal, it's hard to keep a close eye on meats that are cooking over direct heat. They might be burning while you're brewing sweet tea or mixing up the potato salad. The foil wrapper helps prevent that.

NORTH CAROLINA

SMOKY COUNTRY-STYLE RIBS

SERVES 4-6

COOK TIME: 2 HOURS, 30 MINUTES

While these Carolina-style ribs have the notable zing and zang from the vinegar, they offer up a little something extra with the addition of brown sugar, chili sauce, liquid smoke, lemon juice.

INGREDIENTS

- 4 pounds country-style ribs
- Garlic salt, to taste
- Fresh ground pepper, to taste
- 1¼ cup ketchup
- ¾ cup brown sugar, firmly packed
- ½ cup chili sauce
- 2 tablespoons vinegar
- 2 tablespoons liquid smoke seasoning
- 1 tablespoon lemon juice

DIRECTIONS

1. Sprinkle ribs with garlic salt and pepper.

2. Combine remaining ingredients in medium saucepan. Cook over medium heat for about 10 minutes, stirring occasionally. Keep warm.

3. Place ribs, rib bones down, on a rack in a shallow roasting pan. Baste with sauce. Bake at 325°F for 1½– 2 hours, turning and basting with sauce every 30 minutes. Cut into serving portions.

4. Heat remaining sauce and serve with ribs.

TOMATILLOS, JALAPEÑO, AND MEZCAL CAROLINA BBQ STREET TACOS

SERVES 7+

PREP TIME: 1 HOUR | COOK TIME: 4 HOURS

KIMMIE SMITH | NEW YORK, NEW YORK

Growing up and even now, there's nothing like enjoying a tailgate, birthday party, or gathering that's centered around great food and the memories that are made there. Barbecue is an any-season treat, but I'm someone who likes to find a way to take a classic dish and switch it up with tomatillos, poblanos, jalapeños, limes, and mezcal! I love tacos and having them with chicken, lamb, steak, etc., I wanted to create this recipe as an alternative to what we think of in barbecue and to add spices and ingredients that present a new flavor profile! This was largely created based on ingredients that I'm always excited about eating and I love how herbaceous it is! This recipe comes from my love of mezcal and tomatillos. I wanted to create a twist on barbecue with aspects of what makes the Carolina style so great. There's nothing better than a taco and to be able to harness these flavors in your preferred hard or soft tortillas!

INGREDIENTS

BARBECUE SAUCE:
- 1 pound (about 8 medium) tomatillos, husked
- 1 small onion, quartered
- 1 poblano pepper, seeded and diced
- 1 jalapeño pepper, diced
- 3 cups apple cider vinegar
- ½ cup mezcal (I used Mezcal Gracias a Dios)
- ¼ cup honey
- ¼ cup light brown sugar, packed
- 2 teaspoons vegetable oil
- 2 teaspoons kosher salt
- 1 teaspoon ground coriander
- 1 teaspoon dried mustard powder
- 2 teaspoons garlic powder
- ½ teaspoon black pepper
- ½ teaspoon cayenne pepper
- ⅓ tablespoon smoked paprika
- 1 tablespoon sweet and spicy seasoning (I used Tajín)
- 1 teaspoon hot sauce (I used Cholula Green Pepper Hot Sauce)
- 1 teaspoon lime juice

- 1 bunch fresh cilantro, stems and leaves separated

WATERMELON, MANGO, AND CUCUMBER CHOW CHOW:
- 1 cup of water
- 1 cup granulated sugar
- 1 cup dried hibiscus
- 1½ pounds of watermelon, (rind removed), cut into ½-inch pieces (about 3 cups)
- 1 mango, peeled and finely diced
- ½ cup finely diced and seeded English cucumber
- ¼ cup finely diced red onion
- ¼ cup jalapeños, finely diced
- ¼ cup pickled jalapeño brine
- 1 teaspoon lime juice

TACOS:
- 1½ pounds flank steak, sliced thin
- 10 small corn or flour tortillas
- Cotija cheese or haloumi
- Sliced avocados
- Purple cabbage, to taste
- Fresh cilantro, to taste

DIRECTIONS

BARBECUE SAUCE:

1. Preheat your oven to 425°F. Toss the tomatillos and small quartered onions in a bowl with 1 teaspoon of the oil and a sprinkle of salt. Transfer this to a sheet pan and roast in the oven until the vegetables blister and collapse, about 25 minutes.

2. Heat the remaining teaspoon of oil in a medium saucepan over medium-high heat and cook the jalapeños and poblanos until soft (about 3 minutes). Add the honey, apple cider vinegar, brown sugar, coriander, dried mustard powder, garlic powder, black pepper, cayenne pepper, paprika, sweet and spicy seasoning, hot sauce, lime juice, roasted tomatillos and onions, and cilantro stems, and bring to a simmer. Simmer until the sauce is slightly reduced and the roasted onions are very tender (about 20 minutes).

3. Transfer the sauce to a blender, adding the cilantro leaves and salt, and blend until smooth. Season with more salt if desired. Use immediately or refrigerate in a container for no more than 2 days.

WATERMELON, MANGO, AND CUCUMBER CHOW CHOW:

1. Prepare the hibiscus simple syrup by adding the sugar and water to a small saucepan over medium heat. Cook, stirring until sugar is dissolved. Off heat, stir in the hibiscus, and let steep for at least 15 minutes. Strain into a glass jar and seal tightly with a lid. (Hibiscus simple syrup will keep, refrigerated, for about 1 month and is great in cocktails or seltzer.)

2. In a bowl or a quart container, combine the watermelon, mango, cucumber, onion, and jalapeños. Mix until thoroughly combined.

3. Add jalapeño brine, lemon juice, and ¼ cup of the hibiscus simple syrup to the watermelon mixture and mix to combine.

4. Serve immediately as a condiment on the side to enjoy with chips or as a garnish.

TACOS:

1. Take the flank steak and pat dry with paper towels.

2. Place the steak in a single layer in a snug dish. Drizzle the barbecue sauce evenly over the steak, turning to evenly coat. Cover and refrigerate, allowing the steak to marinate for at least 1 hour (but no more than 12 hours), then bring it to room temperature for 30 minutes before cooking.

3. Grease clean grill grates and preheat the grill to 450°F. Grill the steak undisturbed with the lid closed for 5–7 minutes per side. Drizzle and brush with barbecue sauce when turning.

4. Continue to cook steak until cooked through and it reaches 130–135°F for medium-rare.

5. Remove from grill. Cover with foil and allow to rest for 10 minutes.

6. Slice the steak into slices. Using a microwave, skillet, or oven, char on the grill or open gas stovetop flame the small corn tortillas (10) until warm but still pliable. If you are doubling up your tortillas for each taco, then you will need to use 20.

7. Assemble your tacos by layering warmed corn tortilla with red cabbage, barbecued steak slices, sliced avocado, and Cotija cheese.

8. Drizzle with additional barbecue sauce and a squeeze of lime. Garnish with fresh cilantro and limes, if desired. Enjoy!

OTHER REGIONS

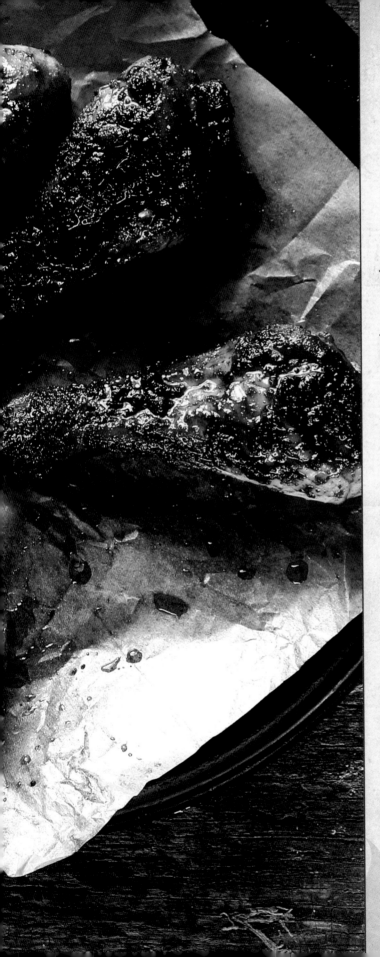

As everyone knows, barbecue isn't exclusive to just the regions we may think of. People all across the United States (and in a later section, the world) love barbecue and know their way around a grill or smoker. The following recipes provide that you don't have to be from Texas to make a mean barbecue dish.

SOUTH CENTRAL
BANDIT'S OKLAHOMA FRIED ONION BURGER

WEST COAST
CALIFORNIA SANTA MARIA TRI-TIP WITH CHIMICHURRI VERDE

NORTHWEST PENNSYLVANIA
COWBOY CANDY MAC

NEW JERSEY
DOUBLE-SMOKED HAM WITH A BOURBON AND BROWN SUGAR GLAZE

HAWAII
HULI-HULI GRILLED CHICKEN

MONTANA
JUICY SMOKED BURGERS

WEST COAST
MONKEY BITE BROWN SUGAR BLUEBERRY OVEN BBQ CHICKEN THIGHS

REVERSE SEARED TRI-TIP WITH CHIMICHURRI

MIDWEST
WAYWAYAWESOME'S SMOKED PORK SANDWICH

Recipes with this symbol represent a gluten-free dish.

BANDIT'S OKLAHOMA FRIED ONION BURGER

SERVES 4

PREP TIME: 45 MINUTES | COOK TIME: 15 MIN

TROY CAMP | BREA, CALIFORNIA

I first heard of the Oklahoma Fried Onion Burger while visiting family in a different state. After eating about four of them, I returned home and instantly started making them for myself. It's a very simple recipe that's ready in about 20 minutes. Over the years of making this recipe, we got the flavors and technique down, and can bring a little bit of Oklahoma to everyone!

INGREDIENTS

- 1 pound $^{80}/_{20}$ ground beef
- 2 white onions
- ½ stick butter (I used Kerrygold)
- 2 tablespoons French onion dip
- 2 tablespoons mustard
- 3–4 dashes Worcestershire sauce
- Hamburger buns
- Cheddar cheese
- 1 tablespoon kosher salt
- Favorite beef seasoning

DIRECTIONS

1. Slice the onions paper thin, then place them into a colander. Salt the onions and them let sit for 30 minutes.
2. Place the onions onto a paper towel and dry as much as possible.
3. Take the ground beef and divide it into four equal-size balls.
4. Get a cast-iron or griddle very hot and melt the butter.
5. Place the burger balls on cast-iron/griddle and use burger press to smash as thin as possible, then place handful of onion slices on patties.
6. Let the burger cook for 2–3 minutes and season.
7. Place a spatula under the burger and, putting a hand on top of onions, flip and cook for another 2–3 minutes.
8. Place the bottom bun on burger to steam and get the onion flavor into it (1 minute). Remove the bun and add cheddar cheese and place the bottom bun back on the heat.
9. Use a spatula to flip the burger (use your hand to hold bottom bun).
10. In a small bowl, mix French onion dip, mustard, and Worcestershire sauce together.
11. Place the spread on the top bun. Place it on burger and enjoy!

CALIFORNIA SANTA MARIA TRI-TIP

SERVES 4

WITH CHIMICHURRI VERDE

PREP TIME: 1 HOUR 45 MINUTES | COOK TIME: 45 MINUTES

HARRY SOO | DIAMOND BAR, CALIFORNIA

I used this recipe to win the KCBS Santa Maria Tri-Tip Championship in Santa Maria, California.

Wood Affects the Flavor of Barbecued Food

One of the nerdiest pieces of barbecue grilling trivia is that if you use wood to grill your food, it's important to choose the right type. Mesquite, hickory, maple, guava, cherry, pecan, apple, and oak are all okay. But you should avoid conifer trees as they release tar and resin and affect the flavor.

Scan QR Code to watch a demonstration of the stealth bomber technique.

INGREDIENTS

MEAT:
- 1 prime grade tri-tip
- 4 tablespoons Worcestershire sauce
- 2 tablespoons salt, pepper, garlic rub (I used Slap Yo Daddy BBQ Santa Maria Rub and Slap Yo Daddy Umami Bomb)

CHIMICHURRI SAUCE:
- 4 tablespoons chopped Italian parsley
- 4 tablespoons chopped cilantro
- 4 cloves garlic, chopped
- 1 tablespoon dried chili flakes, or to taste
- 1 tablespoon dried oregano
- ⅓ cup extra virgin olive oil
- ⅙ cup white vinegar
- 1 teaspoon salt, to taste

DIRECTIONS

1. Trim the tri-tip of excess silver skin facia and fat.
2. Apply Worcestershire sauce and allow it to soak into tri-tip. Reapply as needed.
3. Apply a medium-heavy coat of salt, pepper, and garlic rub (40% salt, 40% pepper, 20% granulated garlic).
4. Rest, if you have time.
5. Smoke the tri-tip at 275°F using live coastal oak, a species of red oak found in the region between Los Angeles and San Francisco. As an alternate, use post oak with hickory, or straight pecan.
6. When the tri-tip is 110°F, sear and char to your preference.
7. Remove when the internal temp is 130°F and let rest to allow temperature to rise to 135°F.
8. Slice and serve following my stealth bomber technique.

CHIMICHURRI SAUCE

1. While the tri-tip is smoking, make the Chimichurri Sauce by combining extra virgin olive oil, vinegar, and salt to taste.
2. Add garlic, cilantro, parsley, and oregano.
3. Add chili flakes to taste.

COWBOY CANDY MAC

SERVES 7+

PREP TIME: 1 HOUR | COOK TIME: 6+ HOURS

JON YORK | ANDOVER, OHIO

This is a menu item at our restaurant that was created a little by mistake. It was created as we were testing recipes for a beef category submission for a barbecue contest. It is going to be the true labor of love because we will be smoking a brisket to start the recipe. I started making brisket about 5 years ago and then created my own version of brisket burnt ends—that candy-like caramelization on a juicy cube of brisket.

INGREDIENTS

BRISKET:
- 10 pounds beef brisket, trimmed or 7 pounds brisket flat
- ½ cup mustard or mustard-based barbecue sauce (i.e. Russell's Dam Good Carolina Sauce)
- 4–6 ounces beef rub (I used Russell's Dam Good Beef Rub), or see Homemade Beef Rub recipe
- 2 cups au jus or beef base
- 2 cups brown sugar
- 2 cups sweet barbecue sauce (I use Russell's Dam Good Sasquatch Sauce), or see Homemade Sweet BBQ Sauce recipe

COWBOY CANDY MAC:
- 2 pounds macaroni, any style of choice
- 1 pound cheddar cheese or any cheese of choice
- 1 pound American cheese, sliced
- 2 cups whole or evaporated milk
- 1 tablespoon dry rub (I used Russell's Dam Good

Butt Rub) or see Homemade Dry Rub recipe
- 1 yellow onion, finely diced
- 1 jalapeño or hot pepper, finely diced

HOMEMADE BEEF RUB
- 1 ounce black pepper
- 1 ounce kosher salt
- ½ ounce garlic powder
- ½ ounce onion powder

HOMEMADE SWEET BARBECUE SAUCE
- 4 cups ketchup
- 1 cup brown sugar
- 1 cup apple cider vinegar
- 1 cup maple syrup
- 1 tablespoon paprika
- 1 tablespoon salt
- 1 teaspoon black pepper
- 1 teaspoon onion
- 1 teaspoon garlic

HOMEMADE DRY RUB
- 1 teaspoon paprika
- 1 teaspoon garlic powder
- 1 teaspoon onion
- 1 teaspoon mustard powder

DIRECTIONS

BRISKET:
1. Start your smoker of choice to 225°F–250°F. I prefer hardwood lump charcoal with some pecan or hickory chunks.
2. Use mustard as a binder on your brisket, then heavily apply beef rub. Let rest for 15 minutes.
3. Put the brisket into a full-size foil pan with beef broth or au jus. Put the pan directly on smoker for 2 hours with fat side facing up.
4. After 2 hours or when internal temperature reaches 145°F, take the brisket out of the pan and put directly on the smoker grates.
5. Flip after 30 minutes to create bark on both sides.
6. Approximately 3 hours in, or when internal temperature reaches 155°F, wrap entire brisket in butcher paper. If you don't have butcher paper, put back into foil pan and cover with foil.
7. Pull brisket off smoker approximately 6 hours later or when internal temperature reaches 195°F.
8. Rest for 1–2 hours at room temp.

COWBOY CANDY MAC:
1. While the brisket is resting, boil the macaroni. While still hot after straining dump it into a full-size foil pan.
2. Add cheese, milk, and seasoning.
3. Cover in foil and put on smoker at 250°F or in oven at 300°F for 30 minutes.
4. Remove foil and stir. Put back on smoker or oven uncovered for 20 minutes or until cheese is melted.
5. Put the diced onion and jalapeño into a foil pan. Dump some of your brisket juice or drippings and put it onto the smoker.
6. Once sauteed, pull off the smoker and add barbecue sauce and brown sugar.
7. Slice the brisket into ½-inch pieces, then cube it into ½-inch cubes.

8. Add cubes into pan with onion, jalapeño, sugar, and sauce.

9. Put back on the smoker at 275°F–300°F for 30–45 minutes or until brisket starts to caramelize.

ASSEMBLY:

1. Put a good couple scoops of mac and cheese in a bowl or plate.

2. Top with a heaping amount of the brisket burnt ends.

3. Drizzle barbecue sauce

4. Add a pinch of barbecue rub.

Optional: Add a pinch of finely diced jalapeño for color.

DOUBLE-SMOKED HAM

SERVES 7+

WITH A BOURBON AND BROWN SUGAR GLAZE

PREP TIME: 30 MINUTES | COOK TIME: 2 HOURS

RAY SHEEHAN | NEW EGYPT, NEW JERSEY

A twice-smoked ham is a pre-cooked ham that is smoked on the grill or in a smoker to infuse it with even more texture and flavor. This is an easy-to-follow process that will get your friends and family excited for their invitation to your next holiday meal.

INGREDIENTS

GLUTEN FREE

HAM:
- One 8–10-pound spiral sliced ham
- ¼ cup yellow mustard
- ¼ cup barbecue rub (I used Plowboys Yardbird Rub)

BOURBON BROWN SUGAR GLAZE:
- 1 cup dark brown sugar, packed
- 2 tablespoons yellow mustard
- ¼ cup bourbon (I used Kentucky Bourbon)
- 1 tablespoon honey
- 1 teaspoon minced garlic
- ⅛ teaspoon cayenne pepper

DIRECTIONS

1. Prepare a smoker to cook at 275°F.
2. Rub the mustard all over the ham and season it with the rub, getting some in between the slices for added flavor, and let it sit for 30 minutes.
3. In a small bowl, stir together the brown sugar, mustard, bourbon, honey, garlic, and cayenne.
4. Brush ½ of the brown sugar mixture evenly over ham.
5. Once the cooker reaches temperature, place the ham in a small pan on the grate in the smoker. Cook for 1½ hours, then brush with the remaining brown sugar mixture.
6. Return the ham to the smoker and continue to cook until it reaches an internal temperature of 140°F, about 30–40 minutes.
7. Remove the ham from the smoker and let rest, loosely covered with foil for 15 minutes.
8. To carve the ham, turn the ham on its bottom so the meat is facing up. Using a long knife, cut around the bone. Then, cut through the natural breaks in the ham where the fat lies to separate the meat.
9. Arrange the ham slices on a platter to serve.

HULI-HULI GRILLED CHICKEN

SERVES 4

PREP TIME: 1 HOUR | COOK TIME: 45 MINUTES

ROB REINHARDT | REGINA, SASKATCHEWAN, CANADA

In the winter of 2021, when our catering business was still decimated by the COVID-19 pandemic, we needed to keep revenue flowing through the cold Canadian winter. We started running weekly take-out specials, with a different theme each week. Since international travel was still discouraged, we thought a tropical theme was in order in the middle of January. This Huli-Huli Grilled Chicken recipe was created, and it has since become one of the most popular food truck specials we have!

INGREDIENTS

HULI-HULI GRILLED CHICKEN:
- 8 boneless chicken thighs (skin is optional)
- Any all-purpose barbecue rub or seasoned salt

HULI-HULI SAUCE:
- 2 teaspoons kosher salt
- ½ teaspoon freshly ground pepper
- 1 cup pineapple juice
- 1 tablespoon light soy sauce
- ¼ cup packed brown sugar
- ⅓ cup ketchup
- ¼ cup chicken broth
- 1 tablespoon sriracha sauce
- 1 teaspoon granulated dry garlic
- 2 teaspoons freshly grated ginger

DIRECTIONS

HULI-HULI SAUCE:
1. Whisk all the ingredients in a sauce pot and heat to a light simmer.
2. Keep simmering until the texture thickens, about 30 minutes.

HULI-HULI GRILLED CHICKEN:
1. Season the chicken thighs with any all-purpose barbecue rub, or lightly season with seasoned salt.
2. Grill over direct medium heat at 350–400°F.
3. Flip the chicken on the grill after 5 minutes and continue cooking for 5–10 minutes until internal temperature reaches 160°F.
4. Baste the chicken with the Huli-Huli barbecue sauce on both sides, and continue grilling until internal temperature reaches 180°F.
5. Remove the chicken from the grill and serve.
6. Save the extra sauce for dipping at the table.

JUICY SMOKED BURGERS

PREP TIME: 15 MINUTES | COOK TIME: 45 MINUTES

HILDA STERNER | MONTANA

The local pub down the street makes the best smoked burgers. Unfortunately, they're only available one day a week during the summer months. For this reason, I decided to come up with my own smoked burgers recipe, which I published on my blog. These smoked burgers are tender, juicy, and have the perfect thickness. I like to serve them piled high with caramelized onions or sautéed morel mushrooms!

INGREDIENTS

- 30 ounces ground beef (20% fat)
- 1 tablespoon kosher salt
- Freshly ground black pepper, to taste
- 6 slices cheese of your choice
- 6 sesame seed buns
- 3 tablespoons butter, softened
- Your favorite burger condiments (ketchup, mayonnaise, mustard, barbecue sauce)
- **Optional toppings:** sliced tomatoes, onions, lettuce, caramelized onions, sautéed mushrooms, bacon

DIRECTIONS

1. Preheat the smoker to 225°F with super smoke option on.
2. Divide ground beef into 5-ounce portions. Form into 6 hamburgers about 5 inches in diameter that are ½-inch thick. Do not over work the meat. Use your thumb to make a dent in the center of each burger.
3. Season burgers with salt and pepper, then transfer onto the heated grill. Stick a probe into the side of one of the burgers, close lid, and set probe temperature to 130°F. It can take anywhere from 30–45 minutes to get to 130°F.
4. Remove the burgers and cover with foil. Turn temperature on the grill up to 450°F. Meanwhile, butter each side of the hamburger buns with softened butter.
5. When the smoker is ready, sear the hamburgers for 2 minutes on each side or until the burgers' internal temperature is 145°F for medium. Top the burgers with cheese during the last 2 minutes. This is also a good time to toast the buttered burger buns.
6. Serve the smoked burgers with an assortment of condiments and toppings for your guests to pick from!

The Perfect Side

The perfect side to ribs, burgers, and dogs is Bush's Baked Beans, of course. My favorite thing to do is heat them up on a pot on the grill. It gives those beans an even better smoky flavor.

MONTANA

MONKEY BITE BROWN SUGAR BLUEBERRY OVEN BBQ CHICKEN THIGHS

SERVES 4

PREP TIME: 15 MINUTES | COOK TIME: 1 HOUR, 15 MINUTES
AVA MARIE ROMERO | SOUTH SAN FRANCISCO, CALIFORNIA

For this recipe, I was inspired to make it because of *Saturday Night Live* alum Chris Kattan and his Mango and Mr. Peepers sketches. This recipe will make a monkey bone out of you with my brown sugar culinary kiss. This recipe is very accessible to families, but worth the wait.

INGREDIENTS

MONKEY BITE BROWN SUGAR SPICE RUB:
- 3 tablespoons brown sugar
- 2 tablespoons ground coffee (I used Monkey Bite Espresso by Bird Rock Coffee Roasters)
- ½ teaspoon sriracha seasoning (I used Kirkland Signature Sriracha Seasoning)
- 1 teaspoon all-purpose seasoning (I used Emeril's Original Essence)

BLUEBERRY BARBECUE SAUCE:
- 1 pound fresh blueberries, washed and rinsed
- 1½ cup low sugar ketchup
- 2 cups brown sugar
- ¾ cup agave nectar
- 2 teaspoons sriracha sauce
- 2 tablespoons ground ginger

CHICKEN THIGHS:
- 1½ pounds boneless skinless chicken thighs
- Salt, to taste

DIRECTIONS

1. Preheat your oven to 375°F. Line a sheet pan with parchment paper and set aside.
2. In a bowl, mix the ingredients for the Monkey Bite Brown Sugar Spice Rub and set aside.
3. In a small saucepan over medium heat, combine Blueberry Barbecue Sauce ingredients bring to a boil. Reduce heat and simmer for 30 minutes or until reduced and thick. Allow to cool completely, then set ½ cup aside to baste with chicken.
4. Place the chicken thighs onto a parchment-lined baking dish. Wash your hands. Season the chicken with a spice rub, wash your hands again, and baste with barbecue sauce.
5. Place in the preheated oven for 25 minutes, basting every 10 minutes or until golden brown on both sides and cooked through. Arrange on a platter and serve family style.

REVERSE SEARED TRI-TIP

SERVES 3

WITH CHIMICHURRI

PREP TIME: 15 MINUTES | COOK TIME: 2 HOURS
CORY SHACKLEFORD | SACRAMENTO, CALIFORNIA

A staple in California, tri-tip and chimichurri is
something we all ate as kids and still love to this
day! The flavor from the beef and chimichurri go
perfect together!

INGREDIENTS

TRI-TIP:
- 2½ pounds tri-tip
- Olive oil, for binding
- Rub of choice (I used a brisket-style rub)

CHIMICHURRI:
- 1 head parsley (about 2 cups copped)
- ½ head cilantro (about 1 cup chopped)
- 1 shallot (about ¼ cup chopped)
- 4 garlic cloves
- 1 tablespoon red pepper flakes
- Juice of ½ lime
- ½ cup red wine vinegar
- ¼ cup olive oil

DIRECTIONS

1. Add a little olive oil to your tri-tip as a binder and
   season with your rub of choice.
2. Let the meat rest for 20 minutes to let the seasoning
   set in.
3. Add to your smoker at 225°F and let it ride until 135°F
   internal temperature. It should take about 1 hour and
   15–30 minutes.
4. While that smokes, make chimichurri by chopping
   parsley, cilantro, shallot, and garlic.
5. Add to a bowl with red pepper flakes, lime juice, red wine vinegar, and olive oil. Stir
   to combine.
6. Once desired temperature on your tri-tip is reached, remove and let rest for 10 minutes.
7. Sear over direct heat to get that beautiful crust.
8. Rest your tri-tip for 10 minutes.
9. Slice, dip in the chimichurri, and enjoy!

HOT TIP

*If you're using a gas
grill, make a smoking
packet by adding wood
chips into a foil pouch
and poking holes on
top to vent.*

WAYWAYAWESOME'S SMOKED PORK SANDWICH

SERVES 7+

COOK TIME: 6+ HOURS

WAYLON LANGSTON | SAINT PAUL, MINNESOTA

My stepdad made pork in a smoker, but I didn't want pork on its own, so I made it into a sandwich! My parents were proud of my sandwich recipe. I would make it every time we smoked pork and I still do. I later would add a special sauce, and I think it tastes great. It's best to make when you have time on a weekend or day off. I really enjoy it, and I hope you do, too!

INGREDIENTS

- 6 pounds pork shoulder
- Steak seasoning, enough to coat entire pork shoulder (I used Fleet Farm Steak Seasoning)
- Hickory wood chips
- ½ cup apple juice
- ½ cup apple cider vinegar
- 2 slices of bread per sandwich (I used Texas Toast)
- Pickles

SPECIAL SAUCE:

- ⅓ cup mayonnaise
- 2 tablespoons barbecue sauce
- 1 tablespoon mustard
- ½ teaspoon buffalo wing sauce

DIRECTIONS

1. Set an electric smoker to 235°F. Season the pork shoulder with the steak seasoning. Put pork shoulder in smoker with hickory wood chips.
2. Occasionally check on it for 3 hours.
3. After 3 hours, reduce heat to 215°F and mist with equal parts apple juice and apple cider vinegar. Continue smoking for another 3 hours until pork has reached 145°F internal temperature.
4. Let rest for 10–15 minutes.
5. Slice pork to your desired thickness.
6. Toast the bread, then build with pork. **Optional: Add barbecue sauce between slices.**
7. Add pickles.
8. Make the Special Sauce: Combine mayo, barbecue sauce, mustard, and buffalo wing sauce.
9. Spread on the special sauce.
10. Enjoy!

What Type of Wood Gives the Best Flavor?

Well, it depends on what you like!

Hickory: My personal favorite but be warned . . . it has a stronger flavor than the others. If you love the taste and smell, but don't want to be overwhelmed, mix it with other woods.

Oak: Has been described as a "medium earthy smoke." I don't know about that, but it is delicious. Oak burns hotter and longer than other woods.

Pecan: As a Georgia boy, I always love my pecans! Tends to bring a sweeter, nuttier flavor to your grilled foods.

INTERNATIO

As mentioned in the earlier chapters of this book, the history of barbecue spans far and wide across the globe. The following recipes are a celebration of international cuisines and how they do barbecue.

KOREA

BAO BUNS WITH SWEET AND SOUR GLAZED BACON

SPICY KOREAN PORK SANDWICH

CANADA

GRILLED PEAMEAL BACON & BEER PANCAKE CUPS

GRILLED WILD BOAR (OR PORK) CHOPS ON APPLE CHERRY ROSEMARY RELISH

IRAN

JOOJEH KABABS

SOUTH KOREA

KING SHORT RIBS

PUERTO RICO/CARIBBEAN

PINCHOS DE POLLO (GRILLED PUERTO RICAN-STYLE CHICKEN SKEWERS)

LATIN AMERICA

PORK BARBACOA OR "PORKACOA" TACOS

JAPAN

PORK BELLY WITH MAPLE SYRUP & SOYA

KOREA-US FUSION

SAN FRANCISCO RIBS WITH BAO BUNS & PICKLED VEGGIES

VIETNAM

VIETNAMESE BBQ PORK SKEWERS (THỊT XIÊN NƯỚNG)

NAL

BAO BUNS

SERVES 4

WITH SWEET AND SOUR GLAZED BACON

PREP TIME: 6+ HOURS | COOK TIME: 2 HOURS

SIMON VANBECELAERE THE BBQ BASTARD | HEULE, BELGIUM

This recipe is an expression of my love for Korean cuisine and my passion for combining diverse flavors. With a preference for Gochujang and being inspired by local street food discoveries, this recipe puts a unique twist on the beloved bao buns. This dish blends simplicity and refinement, ideal for those seeking that extra touch with their side dishes.

The inspiration for this recipe stemmed from a visit to the local street food restaurant, Calavera, where I first tasted bao buns. Calavera is a cozy restaurant with fantastic cocktails and worldly food-sharing dishes, all set in a beautiful environment where children can play peacefully while parents enjoy delicious food. Motivated by their flavorful approach, I decided to create my own version. My passion for cooking and flavor experimentation led to these delicious Bao Buns with Sweet and Sour Glazed Bacon.

What makes these buns special is not only the taste, but also the process behind their creation. The respect for Korean culinary tradition is reflected in the use of ingredients like Gochujang, resulting in a balanced flavor. This recipe embodies my love for Korean flavors and my journey into the world of street food. It's my hope that this dish inspires others to explore flavors and enjoy a unique culinary experience.

INGREDIENTS

- 1½ pounds pork belly slices
- 8 bao buns (Note: Can be homemade or store bought. Ingredients and recipe included below.)
- Fried shallots, for garnish
- Cilantro, for garnish

BAO BUNS:

- 1 tablespoon + 1 teaspoon active yeast
- 5 ounces room temperature water
- 6½ ounces milk
- 1 pound bao flour or all-purpose flour
- 6 tablespoons granulated sugar
- 3 tablespoons non-fat milk powder
- 1 tablespoon salt
- ½ teaspoon baking powder
- ½ teaspoon baking soda
- 2 ounces sunflower oil + some extra for folding

PICKLED CUCUMBER:

- 1 cucumber
- 1 cup water
- 1 cup white sugar
- ¾ cup vinegar, such as rice vinegar
- 1 tablespoon salt

MARINADE:

- 1 tablespoon Chinese five spice
- 2 tablespoons fish sauce
- 2 tablespoons olive oil

SWEET AND SOUR GLAZE:

- 1 tablespoon Gochujang
- 2 cloves garlic
- 1 small piece ginger
- 2 tablespoons fish sauce
- 4 ounces ketchup
- 4 ounces rice vinegar
- 4 tablespoons brown sugar
- 2 tablespoons lime juice

DIRECTIONS

BAO BUNS:

1. Take a deep mixing bowl or a stand mixer and add the flour, milk powder, baking powder, baking soda, and salt. Mix the ingredients well.

2. Attach the dough hook to your stand mixer and activate it at the lowest setting. While the dough hook is mixing, gradually add the water with activated yeast, the milk, and finally the oil.

3. Let it knead for about 10 minutes until a dough ball forms around the hook that doesn't stick too much.

4. Grease a deep bowl with some oil and place the dough in it. Cover with a dry towel and place it at room temperature to rise until the dough has doubled in size, about 1 hour 30 minutes.

5. Place the dough on a clean work surface. Flatten it and divide the dough into 2 equal parts.

6. Divide these parts into about 5 balls of the same size. Gently roll these into a log shape and make balls of approximately the size of a ping pong ball. Place the balls on parchment paper and let them rest under plastic wrap for about half an hour.

7. Place some oil in a small bowl and prepare a "chopstick." Also, prepare some parchment paper sheets where you can place the formed bao buns once folded.

8. Flatten the balls one by one with the palm of your hand and then roll out gently with a lightly greased rolling pin to an oval or circle with a diameter of about 4 inches.

9. Lightly grease the chopstick and place it in the center of the flattened dough. Fold the dough over the stick to form the buns. Remove the chopstick from the dough and place your unbaked bao bun on the parchment paper. Repeat with the other dough balls. Place the finished

buns with enough space between them on the parchment paper and let them rest for another 45 minutes under plastic wrap.

10. Prepare your steam oven or steamer (215°F) and place several bao buns in the steam oven or steamer basket. Steam for 10 minutes.

PICKLED CUCUMBER:

1. Slice the cucumbers into thin slices and place them in a large airtight jar or container.

2. In a separate saucepan, heat water, sugar, vinegar, and salt. Stir until the sugar is completely dissolved.

3. Let the mixture cool to room temperature and pour it over the cucumber slices.

4. Seal the jar or container tightly and refrigerate for at least 12 hours.

MARINADE:

1. Mix the five spice, fish sauce, and olive oil in a large bowl and mix well. Add the pork belly and gently mix to evenly coat the pork with the marinade.

2. Cover the marinade bowl and let the pork marinate in the refrigerator for at least 2 hours and a maximum of 8 hours.

SWEET AND SOUR GLAZE:

1. Finely chop the garlic and grate the ginger.

2. Combine all the ingredients in a medium-large bowl and stir well.

3. Place the sauce over medium-high heat and bring it to a boil. Stir regularly.

4. Let the sauce simmer for 5–7 minutes until the sugar is dissolved and the sauce has thickened.

5. Blend the sauce or strain it through a sieve to filter out any excess bits.

6. Let the sauce cool and use it as a glaze for the pork belly.

BARBECUE:

1. Preheat the barbecue for a low-temperature session (215°F). For an extra smoky touch, place some chunks of cherry wood among the coals or use a pellet smoker tube with cherry wood pellets.

2. Once the smoke is thin and light blue, place the pork belly on the grill.

3. Let the pork cook for about 2 hours until it reaches an internal temperature of approximately 198°F, making it buttery soft.

4. Regularly check around the temperature of 194°F to test if the pork is cooked sufficiently. Depending on the thickness of the pork slices, the time may be shorter or longer.

5. Glaze the pork belly on both sides. Increase the temperature in the barbecue to 365°F and grill the pork briefly (about 3 minutes) to allow the glaze to adhere well to the meat.

FINISHING TOUCHES:

1. Steam the bao buns in the steam oven or your steamer.

2. Place a piece of glazed pork belly in the bao bun along with strips of pickled cucumber.

3. Top with fried shallots and cilantro to taste.

4. Enjoy your meal!

GRILLED PEAMEAL BACON & BEER PANCAKE CUPS

MAKES 12 CUPS

PREP TIME: 10 MINUTES | COOK TIME: 21–24 MINUTES

MADDIE & KIKI | ONTARIO, CANADA

Everyone loves pancakes! So why not take your pancake game to the next level? Turn them into hand-held Grilled Peameal Bacon & Beer Pancake Cups! They are made using beer in the pancake batter and then are loaded with charcoal grilled peameal bacon (aka Canadian Bacon)! As Canadians, we try to eat as much peameal bacon as we can, so serve them for breakfast, brunch, lunch, dinner . . . literally any time of day!

INGREDIENTS

- 6 slices peameal bacon
- 1 cup flour
- 1 tablespoon sugar
- ½ teaspoon baking soda
- 1 teaspoon baking powder
- ½ teaspoon your favorite barbecue rub
- 1 egg
- 1 cup beer
- 2 tablespoons butter, melted
- 1 teaspoon vanilla extract
- 2 green onions, finely sliced
- Avocado oil cooking spray

DIRECTIONS

1. Preheat grill to high heat between 425–450°F.
2. Grill peameal bacon over direct heat until fully cooked to an internal temperature of 145°F, approximately 3–4 minutes per side.
3. Set aside and allow to cool. Cut into small chunks. (Or if you like big chunks, cut into big chunks!)
4. In a bowl, combine the flour with the sugar, baking soda, baking powder, and barbecue rub.
5. In a separate bowl, whisk the egg with the beer, butter, and vanilla.
6. Add the wet ingredients to the dry ingredients and whisk to combine. Gently stir in the green onions.
7. Spray the inside of 12 silicone muffin cups with the avocado oil.
8. Spoon the mixture evenly amongst the cups.
9. Top with the bacon chunks, pushing them into the batter slightly.
10. Place the cups back into the grill (at 450°F) over indirect heat and grill for 18–20 minutes, until a wooden skewer inserted into the center comes out clean. Serve with more green onions, and LOTS of maple syrup!

Scan QR Code to watch.

GRILLED WILD BOAR (OR PORK) CHOPS

ON APPLE CHERRY ROSEMARY RELISH

SERVES 4

PREP TIME: 30 MINUTES | COOK TIME: 45 MINUTES

JANICE SMELLA | CALGARY, ALBERTA, CANADA

I created this recipe as my signature dish in preparation for my debut in a live-fire barbecue cooking TV show, *Fire Masters*. I wanted to create a dish that would be sweet, savory, and different than what other cooks would create. There is versatility with this recipe to substitute pork chops, in lieu of boar chops. Peaches, blueberries, rhubarb or pear can be substituted instead of cherries. This is not your typical barbecue dish that can be found in most barbecue restaurants. The opportunity to use fresh ingredients, in season is important to me. We are so fortunate to be able to grow delicious food in North America and the farmers that supply our markets are passionate and proud of what they grow. This dish encapsulates that passion with my passion for the grill.

Pork and boar is well accentuated with fruit, especially with fresh herbs. I especially love fresh rosemary. Marrying the sweet and savory to compliment and allow the notes to dance on your tongue is the art! This dish showcases everything I love about tying barbecue to the seasons and making it a unique meal that you won't find anywhere else! Alas, I cooked a different recipe on the reality TV cooking show, but this recipe has become a staple in our kitchen. I hope it will become one in yours, too!

INGREDIENTS

- 4 wild boar or pork rib chops (2-inch loin muscle)

RUB:
- 2 tablespoons kosher salt
- 3 teaspoons garlic powder
- 1 teaspoon paprika
- ½ teaspoon cinnamon
- ¼ teaspoon ground nutmeg
- ½ teaspoon cumin
- ½ teaspoon sage

SAUCE:
- 2 tablespoons butter
- 1 medium onion, finely chopped
- 1 garlic clove, minced
- 1 medium Granny Smith apple, peeled and finely chopped
- 2 cups of fresh cherries
- 1–2 tablespoons flour
- 2 cups chicken broth
- 1 tablespoon soy sauce
- 3–4 tablespoons brown sugar
- Sprinkle of red pepper flakes
- 2½ tablespoons finely diced fresh rosemary
- ¼ teaspoon sea salt
- ¼ teaspoon nutmeg

DIRECTIONS

CHOPS:
1. Warm the grill or barbecue to 350°F.
2. Add rosemary to a charcoal grill for smoking.
3. Grill the boar chop slightly.
4. Flip and grill the chop on indirect heat to 135°F.
5. Sizzle and add additional rub on each side. (Total grill time 15–20 minutes.)
6. Let the chop rest and prepare and cook the Apple Cherry Rosemary Relish.

APPLE CHERRY ROSEMARY RELISH:
1. Pit the cherries and set aside.
2. Melt the butter in a frying pan on medium heat.
3. Add onions and garlic and cook them until softened.
4. Add apples and cook until tender.
5. Stir in the flour to create a roux and add additional rub on each side to sizzle and sear. (Total grill time is 15–20 minutes.)
6. Stir in the chicken broth.
7. Add soy sauce, brown sugar, red pepper flakes, fresh diced rosemary, and nutmeg.
8. Add the cherries.
9. Cook the sauce until it coats the back of a spoon or until it reaches the desired consistency.

JOOJEH KABABS

SERVES 4

PREP TIME: 5 HOURS | COOK TIME: 15 MINUTES
FARAZ | IRAN

Every Persian family in Iran is familiar with how to cook grilled chicken, and this dish is prepared at 80% of barbecues. The deliciousness of this dish can be summed up in flavoring the chicken before cooking it. And this process takes about 5 to 7 hours.

INGREDIENTS

- 1½–2 pounds chicken
- 1 medium onion
- 2 large pieces of yogurt extract
- ⅔ cup infused saffron
- 4 tablespoons olive oil
- 4 tablespoons butter
- ⅔ cup fresh ginger
- ⅓ cup lemon juice
- 3 tablespoons salt
- 3 tablespoons black pepper

HOT TIP

If you want your grilled chicken to be soft and delicious without being dry and tough, be sure to add the amount of lime juice in the grilled chicken carefully and don't add too much—it will toughen the meat!

DIRECTIONS

1. Wash the chicken and remove the extra skins, then dice. If you want to prepare grilled chicken for your parties, it is better to use only the breast.

2. After chopping the chicken, put it in a large bowl.

3. Cut the onions into large slices or rings and place between the chopped chicken meat. Of course, if you wish, you can also use onion juice to flavor the chicken meat.

4. Add olive oil and mix well with chicken meat, then add lemon juice along with salt, black pepper, condensed yogurt, and 2 tablespoons of infused saffron to the bowl. Mix with your hands until fully coated.

5. Cover the bowl with cellophane and place in the refrigerator for at least 5 hours so that the chicken not only rests, but also becomes flavorful. Of course, if you want your grilled chicken to taste like it does in a restaurant, it's best to season the chicken the night before.

6. After the chicken is flavored, take it out of the refrigerator, then place on a flat surface (like a meat board). Holding each piece of chicken meat with your hand, pass a skewer through it. Note: For skewering, it's important to consider putting bone parts (such as shoulder and wings) on one skewer, and meat pieces (such as breast meat) on another so that the joojeh kebabs cook evenly.

7. Prepare the charcoal grill. **Note: Be sure to pay attention to whether the coals are completely lit and aren't smoking. The smoke in the coals is not only harmful to the body, but also causes the taste of the kebabs to be smoky.**

8. After the coals are ready, put the chicken skewers on the grill and let the kebabs catch a little, then rotate them continuously so they are evenly grilled. While roasting the chicken, prepare the butter sauce.

9. Melt the butter, then add the rest of the brewed saffron and mix well.

10. After the chicken is completely grilled, apply butter sauce on both sides with a clean brush and let them stay on the heat for another minute.

11. After a minute, take the skewered chicken off the grill and place on a plate. Hold the chicken with your hands, then pull out the skewer.

12. Serve the grilled chicken with bread or rice.

HOT TIP

One of the ingredients used to flavor joojeh kababs is mayonnaise. For the amount of ingredients listed here, mix a cup of mayonnaise with 2 tablespoons of condensed yogurt and use it along with other ingredients to flavor the chicken. By doing this, the taste of the grilled chicken will be different and not everyone may like it, so be sure to taste test before making grilled chicken for your guests with this method!

IRAN

KING SHORT RIBS

SERVES 4

PREP TIME: 7+ HOURS | COOK TIME: 15 MINUTES
THE KOREAN BBQ CHEF | BOULDER, COLORADO

If one were to ask many what their favorite Korean barbecue dish would be, almost everyone would answer with Galbi. This flavorful King Short Ribs dish is what placed Korean barbecue on the map. Our KBC King Galbi recipe has been passed down in our family for generations, receiving positive reactions from first-time Korean barbecue explorers to die-hard KBBQ lovers. It can be quickly marinated and ready to cook to following day. (Give about 24 hours for the sauce and meat to get acquainted with one another!) The ingredients are simple: we find extracting the most natural flavors can be achieved from natural sources. KBC King Galbi pairs well with various side dishes, such as healthy kimchi! All our recipes, including this one, are created with the goal of obtaining umami through healthy eating, and we hope everyone's taste buds can concur!

INGREDIENTS

- 3–4 pounds beef short ribs

MARINADE:
- 1 teaspoon roasted salt
- 1 teaspoon organic cane brown sugar
- 5 tablespoons of Korean pear juice
- 2 tablespoons roasted sesame oil
- 2 teaspoon minced garlic

DIRECTIONS

1. Thinly slice the meat and then create diamond cuts.
2. Mix the marinade ingredients well. For best results, marinate overnight.
3. Preheat the grill on medium-high heat. Grill the meat about 2–3 minutes on each side or to liking.

PINCHOS DE POLLO

SERVES 7+

(GRILLED PUERTO RICAN-STYLE CHICKEN SKEWERS)

PREP TIME: 1 HOUR, 30 MINUTES | COOK TIME: 30 MINUTES

RAMONA CRUZ-PETERS | ROUND ROCK, TEXAS

"Pinchos," which is derived from the Basque word "pintxos," means "skewers" or "spikes." In Spain, the word pintxo is used generally for tapas served on cocktail sticks. Puerto Rican pinchos specifically refer to marinated and barbecued meat kabobs, which also happen to be a popular street food. If you've visited Puerto Rico, you've likely seen street vendors selling pork or chicken pinchos from roadside stands. If you want to relive your memories of Puerto Rico at home, I'm sharing a recipe for homemade grilled pinchos de pollo, using techniques and seasonings passed down to me from my Puerto Rican father.

INGREDIENTS

- Bamboo skewers
- 3 pounds boneless, skinless chicken thighs, cut into bite-size cubes
- 3 tablespoons corn oil, divided
- Two 0.2-ounce packets sazón con culantro y achiote (from a box of multiple packets)
- 2 teaspoons adobo all-purpose seasoning
- 1½ teaspoons dried oregano
- ½ teaspoon garlic powder
- ½ teaspoon ground cumin
- ⅓ cup barbecue sauce
- Baguette, sliced into 1-inch rings

DIRECTIONS

1. Place the bamboo skewers in a dish of warm water to soak until you're ready to use them. Make sure the skewers are completely submerged in the water.

2. Combine chicken cubes, 2 tablespoons corn oil, sazón, adobo, oregano, garlic powder, and cumin in a large container until the seasoning is well blended and the chicken pieces are completely coated. Cover and refrigerate for 1 hour.

3. Remove the marinated chicken from the refrigerator. Remove the skewers from the water and place on paper towels to dry slightly. Slide chicken onto the skewers, leaving space on each end, until you have used all the chicken.

4. Heat a grill to medium heat, then add the chicken to the grill in a single layer. Grill the chicken for 5 minutes, then brush with barbecue sauce before flipping the chicken over and brushing barbecue sauce on the other side. Cook for 5 more minutes, then check chicken for doneness.

5. Brush more barbecue sauce onto the chicken and cook for a few more minutes, or until chicken has reached an internal temperature of 165°F.

6. Brush baguette pieces with the remaining corn oil, then place them on the grill until toasted.

7. Add a piece of toasted bread to the end of each pincho skewer and serve.

PUERTO RICO/CARIBBEAN

PORK BARBACOA OR "PORKACOA" TACOS

SERVES 6

PREP TIME: 6+ HOURS | COOK TIME: 6+ HOURS

MATTHEW FUCHS | SPARTA, NEW JERSEY

In trying to utilize different and cheaper (inflation is real) cuts of meat, I came across a sale from one of my meat purveyors for pork cheeks. I did some basic research and with several failed recipes, I learned that smoking and utilizing the confit process makes the pork cheeks delicious. Tacos were the obvious choice for pork cheeks because of their size (you don't get much meat per cheek). I've made beef barbacoa before for tacos, so I wanted to test the quality between beef and pork. The bonus for pork cheeks is that there is a lot of trim. That trim can be ground down for sausage or made into lardon. Minimizing waste is big for my recipes. You can you can melt down the fat from the trim and use it as the base fat when you begin the confit process.

INGREDIENTS

- 10–20 pounds pork cheeks, untrimmed
- Fajita seasoning, to taste (I used Meat Church Dia de la Fajita Rub)
- Mexican lager (I used Corona)
- 8 cups pork fat or beef tallow
- Texas barbecue rub (kosher salt and 16 mesh)
- Mango salsa (any recipe you can find online will suffice)
- 1 large head lettuce
- 1 white onion
- 1 plum tomato
- 1 bunch cilantro
- Corn tortillas
- One package crumbled Cotija cheese or queso fresco
- Sour cream (optional for topping)

DIRECTIONS

1. Trim the pork down to just the small cheek. Save the trim for freezing for a later date.
2. Marinate overnight with a Mexican lager and light dusting of fajita seasoning and Texas barbecue rub.
3. The next day, pull from the marinade and pat dry with paper towel.
4. Lightly coat with Texas barbecue rub. (Usually, pork can take heavy seasoning, but since the meat pieces are very small, don't go heavy like you would for a brisket or pork shoulder.)
5. Fire your smoker up at 225–250°F using apple wood or post oak. Other woods—such as hickory, pecan, and cherry—are all woods that complement pork nicely.
6. Smoke for 2–4 hours until a mahogany-colored, crusty bark has formed. Depending on the climate, temperature, and the type of smoker you have, it could be done in 2 hours, or take as long as 4 hours. You aren't cooking the pork to doneness, just forming nice bark and color.
7. Pull from the smoker and put into an oven-safe baking dish.
8. Cover with pork fat or beef tallow.
9. Cover with foil and cook for 10 hours at 200°F. (If you're fancy and have the means, utilizing an Alto-Shaam-type oven is a great resource. I have one at the restaurant and it comes out great, but ovens work just fine as well.)
10. Pull from the liquid and let cool.
11. Pull apart with two forks and dice the vegetables and cilantro.
12. Assemble tacos with the lettuce first, then pork mango salsa, onions, tomatoes, cheese, and cilantro. Feel free to add or subtract any ingredients. The joy of tacos is you can make them into whatever you want them to be. The world is yours!

Keep it Simple

When cooking with high-quality meat, often the best "marinade" is simply salt and pepper. When enjoying a prime ribeye or filet mignon, I never add anything except salt and pepper.

PORK BELLY WITH MAPLE SYRUP & SOYA

SERVES 5

PREP TIME: 30 MINUTES | COOK TIME: 5 HOURS

YAKINIKU | ORIGINAL JAPANESE GRILL NETHERLANDS

We've had the pleasure of writing three wonderful books, all inspired by barbecue. One of our books is specifically about kamado and is full of delicious recipes you can prepare on the kamado, from fish to meat and even veggie recipes! One of these recipes is the super tender pork belly, a classic barbecue dish, but with the use of our salt stone grill, gives it a unique flavor that you won't forget! This recipe is one of many recipes from our cookbook, but a typical dish for the kamado that everyone can prepare, whether you're a novice or an experienced chef!

INGREDIENTS

- 2 pounds pork belly (unsalted)
- 3⅓ cups water
- 5 ounces maple syrup
- 3–3½ tablespoons soya sauce

DIRECTIONS

1. Start the kamado with a medium amount of coals and place in the multilevel lift, the heat deflector, and the standard grid. Bring to 355°F. Place the cast-iron pan on the grill so that it heats up along with the kamado.

2. Cut the pork belly into 1-inch-thick pieces and place in the pan when it's hot.

3. Mix the water with the maple syrup and soya sauce. You can play around with the proportions if you want the pork belly to be sweeter or saltier. For this preparation, we're going to lightly fry the pork belly on a salt stone at the end, which is why we're using very little soy.

4. When the pork belly is lightly browned, turn it over and brown the other side as well.

5. Add the gravy and put the lid on the pan. Leave the kamado at 355°F for an hour and then close the bottom draft door almost completely to bring the temperature down. The ideal temperature is around 200°F–205°F.

6. Leave the pork belly to braise in the kamado for 4 hours.

7. Check after 4 hours and if it's not fully cooked, leave it in the kamado for a little longer.

8. Once the pork belly is cooked, remove the pan from the kamado. Also remove the multilevel lift and the heat deflector. Add additional charcoal and bring the kamado up to 480°F.

9. Place the standard grid with the salt stone on top and allow it to heat up thoroughly.

10. Take the pork belly out of the pan and cut it in half again lengthwise so you have about ½-inch slices.

11. Fry briefly on the salt stone and then brush with the gravy left in the pan. Taste, and if it's too salty, add some maple syrup. If it's too sweet, add some soya. If it's too thick, add more water.

JAPAN

SAN FRANCISCO RIBS

WITH BAO BUNS & PICKLED VEGGIES

PREP TIME: 20 MINUTES | COOK TIME: 4 HOURS

JOHN MARDIKIAN | SAN FRANCISCO, CALIFORNIA

This recipe pairs great with my San Francisco BBQ Sauce (page 147). It's a spin on the fusion food movement, which brought together Eastern and Western techniques and ingredients, resulting in a cuisine that captures the best of both styles.

INGREDIENTS

RIBS:
- 2 racks of baby back ribs (about 1½ pounds each)
- San Francisco BBQ Sauce (recipe on page 147)
- Salt, to taste
- Pepper, to taste

BAO BUNS:
- ⅓ cup warm water
- ½ cup warm milk
- 1 tablespoon active dry yeast
- 2 tablespoons sugar
- 2 tablespoons canola oil
- 2½ cups all-purpose flour
- ½ teaspoon baking powder
- ½ teaspoon salt

PICKLED CARROTS AND DAIKON:
- 1 daikon root
- 2 large carrots
- 1 cup white vinegar
- 3 tablespoons sugar
- 1 tablespoon salt

DIRECTIONS

RIBS:
1. Season baby back ribs with salt and pepper and brush with San Francisco BBQ sauce.
2. Wrap each rack in foil and bake in the oven for 3 hours at 275°F.
3. Raise oven to 425°F. Unwrap ribs and brush again with barbecue sauce, roast in the hot oven for 10 minutes.

BAO BUNS
1. Mix milk, water, yeast, and sugar and let it rest for 15 minutes.
2. Combine the yeast mixture with the canola oil, flour, baking powder, and salt in a stand mixer and mix until a dough is formed.
3. Allow dough to rest at room temperature for 1 hour.
4. Roll out dough on a lightly flowered surface to ½-inch thickness.
5. Use a 3-inch round cookie cutter to cut out rounds. Fold them in half and place in a steamer at a rolling boil for 10 minutes.

PICKLED CARROTS AND DAIKON
1. Peel both carrots and daikon.
2. Chop into a fine Julienne cut. I use a mandolin to get the right consistency.
3. Combine with white vinegar, sugar, and salt.
4. Make sure vinegar mix covers the shredded carrots and daikon.
5. Place carrots, daikon, and vinegar mix into a container and ensure that they're submerged.
6. Allow to marinate overnight or at least for a few hours. They can be made days in advance.

ASSEMBLY:
1. Chop fresh cilantro leaves.
2. Cut the racks of ribs into single ribs, then remove the bones (should slide right out).
3. Place the meat, pickled carrots and daikon, and a few leaves of cilantro into each bun and drizzle with San Francisco BBQ Sauce.
4. Enjoy!

SPICY KOREAN PORK SANDWICH

SERVES 7+

PREP TIME: 7 HOURS | COOK TIME: 6 HOURS, 30 MINUTES

JIYEON LEE | ATLANTA, GEORGIA

This sandwich includes a tangy kimchi coleslaw, crunchy pickles, and smoky leftover pork pieces marinated in gochujang on soft potato bun.

INGREDIENTS

PORK:

- 2 cups gochugaru (Korean red pepper flakes)
- 1 cup sweet chili sauce (such as Mae ploy)
- 1 cup sriracha
- 1 cup gochujang (Korean red pepper paste)
- 8 pounds boneless pork butt
- ¼ cup sesame oil

KIMCHI SLAW:

- 1 pound thinly sliced cabbage
- 2 cups thinly Julienned carrots
- 1 cup thinly sliced scallions
- 6 cloves garlic, minced
- ½ cup gochugaru (Korean red pepper flakes)
- ½ cup sugar
- 3 tablespoons salt
- 1 tablespoon ground black pepper
- 2 tablespoons rice vinegar

DIRECTIONS

PORK:

1. Stir together gochugaru, sweet chili sauce, sriracha, and gochujang in a large bowl, leaving a cup of marinade sauce on the side for later. Marinate pork butt by tossing to coat, covering, and let it chill overnight.

2. Prepare the smoker by preheating it to 225°F. When ready, cook the pork for about 4 hours until it's tender and the meat thermometer inserted into thickest portion registers at least 145°F.

3. Remove the pork from smoker and let it stand 20 minutes. Cut into small cubes and drizzle with additional marinade sauce and sesame oil.

KIMCHI SLAW:

1. Mix all the ingredients in a large bowl. Serve fresh.

ASSEMBLE:

1. Toast the bun and assemble sandwich with spicy Korean pork and slaw.

VIETNAMESE BBQ PORK SKEWERS
(THỊT XIÊN NƯỚNG)

PREP TIME: 30 MINUTES | COOK TIME: 15 MINUTES
PEDR FINN | DA NANG, VIETNAM

After going to a street vendor in Hội An many times to enjoy these amazing pork skewers, I finally convinced the 75-year-old woman to share her secret recipe. In Vietnam, they are served with a plate of leafy greens and rice paper. Ordered by the plateful, locals will sit on the busy street corner on little plastic chairs watching the world pass before them. Just pull the meat from the skewer, roll with leafy greens creating a rice paper roll, and dip into sweet Vietnamese fish sauce.

INGREDIENTS

- 1 pound pork belly
- 2 bulbs lemongrass
- 1 red chili
- 3 shallots bulbs
- 3 garlic cloves
- ½ onion
- 1 lime, juiced
- 20 bamboo skewers

MARINADE:
- 1 tablespoon fish sauce
- 2 tablespoons oyster sauce
- 1 teaspoon black pepper
- 1–2 tablespoons condensed milk
- 1–2 teaspoons sesame oil
- 1 tablespoon honey
- 1 tablespoon brown sugar
- 1 tablespoon water

BASTE:
- 1 tablespoon oyster sauce
- 1 tablespoon honey
- 1 tablespoon cooking oil

DIRECTIONS

1. Thinly slice pork belly into 0.5 cm slices lengthwise.

2. Soak bamboo skewers in cold water for about 20–30 minutes. This will prevent them from burning when cooking.

3. In a food processor, place lemongrass, shallots, garlic, juice of lime, red chili, and half an onion and blend into a fine paste.

4. Prepare the sauce for marinating the meat. In a large bowl, add oyster sauce, pepper, condensed milk, honey, fish sauce, sesame oil, brown sugar, water, and the puréed lemongrass mix.

5. After you have prepared the sauce, add sliced pork and mix evenly.

6. Let the meat absorb the spice for at least 3–4 hours. If you have time, cover the bowl with food wrap, place it in the refrigerator and leave overnight.

7. Proceed to skewer all the meat on the bamboo sticks, adjust the skewers of meat neatly and evenly. Note: The meat shouldn't be skewed too thick and pressed too tightly because it will take a lot of time to grill and presents the possibility of the meat burning on the outside before inside is cooked.

8. Keep the remaining marinade and prepare the mixture that will be used to baste the skewers when cooking. Add oyster sauce, honey and cooking oil and mix well.

9. For the best results and flavor, use a charcoal barbecue. However, gas barbecue can also be used.

10. Grill skewers for about 2–4 minutes each side.

11. Using a brush, baste skewers on each side when cooking.

SEAFOOD

When you think of barbecue, you think of meat, but seafood deserves a special shoutout, too! The following recipes are for the foodies who aren't afraid to deviate from the norm and try something that's more unexpected, but still *sea-riously* good!

BARBECUED LOBSTER WITH LIME, GARLIC, AND HERB BUTTER
BBQ OYSTERS
MAPLE CHIPOTLE SALMON
MIXED SEAFOOD KEBABS
OVEN BARBECUED FISH (SAMAK MASHWI)

BARBECUED LOBSTER
WITH LIME, GARLIC, AND HERB BUTTER

SERVES 4

COOK TIME: 5–8 MINUTES

JANE LOVETT | LONDON, ENGLAND

The king of shellfish, lobster isn't cheap, but when bought in season, it's more reasonably priced. Cheaper (and fresher) still, is to buy it directly from fishermen. When buying live lobsters, make sure there are rubber bands around the claws, as they can be vicious. If only larger lobsters are available, buy two and serve half to each person. If barbecuing isn't an option, grill the lobsters instead.

INGREDIENTS

- 4 live lobsters weighing around 1 pound each
- 2 ounces butter
- 3 limes
- 2 cloves garlic, chopped
- 2 tablespoons chopped fresh parsley
- Salt and freshly ground black pepper, to taste

HOT TIP

To prepare ahead of time, follow recipe through to Step #2 any time on the day you are eating the lobsters, cover, and refrigerate.

Live lobsters are better cooked the day of purchase. However, they will keep in the fridge overnight if packed in a container with a damp cloth or newspaper around and on top of them. Don't cover with a lid.

DIRECTIONS

1. Split the lobsters in half from top to bottom by straightening out the tail and inserting the point of a large chopping knife down through the natural cross at the back of the head. It will die instantly. Continue to cut down through the tail and then the rest of the head and split open into two halves. Remove the little sack from the head and the thin black intestine that runs from the head to the tail with the point of a knife. Keep any gooey greenish liver, which is considered a delicacy, and also the roe if there is any, which will be black at this stage.

2. Put the claws between a cloth and crack with a sharp blow from a rolling pin or hammer. Be careful not to shatter them—just a crack or two.

3. Melt the butter and add the zest and juice of 1 lime, garlic, parsley, salt, and pepper.

4. Brush the butter over the lobster, put onto the very hot barbecue, cover with a lid if it has one, and cook for a few minutes until the lobster shells have turned from black to red and the flesh becomes opaque. Brush with more butter mixture during cooking. If your barbecue has no lid, cook flesh-side down for 2–3 minutes, then turn over, brush with more butter, and cook until the shells are red and the flesh is opaque.

5. Serve with fresh or charred lime wedges, crusty bread, and a large green salad.

HOT TIP

When barbecuing, make sure the coals are white hot with a thin coating of ash over the top, before cooking. This will take 40–60 minutes after lighting.

"THE ONLY TIME TO EAT DIET FOOD IS WHILE YOU'RE WAITING FOR THE STEAK TO COOK."

—JULIA CHILD, CHEF, TV PERSONALITY, AND AUTHOR

SEAFOOD

BBQ OYSTERS

SERVES 2

COOK TIME: 10–15 MINUTES

**DERMOT O'LEARY, JAMES GINZLER, AND
PAUL SHOVLIN | LONDON, UNITED KINGDOM**

This is a pretty unconventional way of cooking oysters—we discovered that if you put scrubbed unshucked oysters on a barbecue, they will just pop open when cooked.

INGREDIENTS

- 12 rock oysters

BARBECUE SAUCE:
- 5 tablespoons ketchup
- 1 tablespoon brown sugar
- Pinch cayenne pepper
- Pinch smoked paprika
- ½ shallot, finely chopped
- 1 garlic clove, crushed
- Pinch allspice
- Pinch ground cinnamon
- Pinch ground mace
- Pinch black pepper

DIRECTIONS

1. First make the barbecue sauce. Place all ingredients in a saucepan and heat over a low heat until the sugar has dissolved. Allow to cool and store in an airtight container until needed.

2. If you don't want to barbecue the oysters, shuck them and arrange them in their shells on a baking tray. Drizzle a teaspoon of the barbecue sauce over each one and cook under a hot grill for 2–3 minutes. Alternatively, put them straight on to the barbecue until they steam or pop open.

3. Remove with tongs (the shells will be very hot), then add the sauce to them.

SEAFOOD

MAPLE CHIPOTLE SALMON

SERVES 4

PREP TIME: 15 MINUTES | COOK TIME: 45 MINUTES

ROB REINHARDT | REGINA, SASKATCHEWAN, CANADA

This recipe is one of my signature dishes. It's a simple recipe, developed for the Chef's Choice category at the Jack Daniels World BBQ Championships. I'm proud to say it has won first place at this event on three separate occasions.

INGREDIENTS

- 1 salmon filet, roughly 2–4 pounds
- 3 chipotle peppers from can with adobo sauce (about 2 ounces)
- 1 teaspoon adobo sauce from can
- ⅔ cup maple syrup
- 2 teaspoons salt
- 1 teaspoon pepper

DIRECTIONS

MAPLE CHIPOTLE GLAZE:

1. Slice the chipotle peppers and remove the seeds.
2. Finely chop the peppers.
3. Add the maple syrup to a small pan and heat on the stove.
4. Add the chopped chipotle peppers and adobo sauce to syrup in the pan and whisk together. Bring to a light simmer and turn off the heat.
5. Allow the glaze to cool. It should be lukewarm when it's applied to the fish, but not hot.

SALMON:

1. Heat the smoker or grill to 300°F.
2. Place the salmon on a cedar plank. (If using a gas grill, or a charcoal grill directly above the fire, make sure the plank has been fully submerged in water for 2 hours). If you don't have a cedar plank, you can place the salmon filet directly on the grill. The skin may stick, but that's okay.
3. Season the salmon with salt and pepper.
4. Cook. After 30 minutes, apply the glaze with a silicone brush (or barbecue sauce brush) to the surface of the fish. Repeat every 5 minutes, Two to three coats of the glaze should suffice.
5. After 40–50 minutes in total, the fish should be done. Remove when the fat appears on the surface of the fish and the thickest part of the flesh is opaque and flaky. At this point, the fish is done. The internal temperature should be about 145°F.
6. Serve!

MIXED SEAFOOD KEBABS

MAKES 8 SKEWERS

PREP TIME: 30 MINUTES | COOK TIME: 30 MINUTES
DERMOT O'LEARY, JAMES GINZLER, AND
PAUL SHOVLIN | LONDON, UNITED KINGDOM

These kebabs are great for summer barbecues and make an interesting change from the usual burgers and sausages. Feel free to customize however you like, adding cherry tomatoes, shrimp, and other fixings!

INGREDIENTS

- 1½ pounds mixed white fish, such as pollock or huss
- 4 tablespoons olive oil, plus extra for grilling
- 16 scallops
- 4 red peppers, deseeded and cut into large dice
- 2 red onions, largely diced
- Salt and freshly ground black pepper, to taste

DIRECTIONS

1. Soak eight wooden skewers in water for about 30 minutes to prevent them from burning when you cook the kebabs.

2. Cut the fish into chunks and place in a large bowl, along with the scallops. Drizzle the olive oil over the fish and season.

3. Thread each skewer alternately with the fish, scallops, peppers, and onions until all the ingredients are used up.

4. Place the kebabs on a tray and drizzle the oil left in the bowl over them and chill until you are ready to cook.

5. Rub a little oil on to the barbecue grill and lay the skewers on top.

6. Allow 3–5 minutes each side so the heat can penetrate through the flesh before turning. Each side will need slightly less time than the one before. After 3 or 4 turns, remove the kebabs.

7. Either serve them on the skewers or push all the barbecued ingredients into a big bowl for sharing.

OVEN BARBECUED FISH

(SAMAK MASHWI)

SERVES 6

PREP TIME: 15 MINUTES | COOK TIME: 1 HOUR

MARIA KHALIFÉ | BEIRUIT, LEBANON

Samak Mashwi translates to "grilled fish" in Arabic and is a beloved Middle Eastern dish, especially in Lebanon, Syria, Jordan, and Palestine. Its history dates back to ancient times when fishermen would cook their fresh catches over open fires on the shores of the Mediterranean Sea. Preparing the fish this way was a practical way to cook seafood, but also enhanced its fresh, natural flavors. Enjoy this timeless dish and serve with a side salad, rice, lemon slices, or vegetables!

INGREDIENTS

- 1 whole perch, trout, or carp weighing about 3½ pounds
- 4 tablespoons vegetable oil
- 3 large onions, peeled and thinly sliced
- 5 garlic cloves, peeled and crushed
- 1 teaspoon curry powder
- 1 teaspoon ground dried lime or grated rind of 1 lemon
- 2 teaspoons salt
- 2 tablespoons tamarind paste
- 1 cup warm water
- 3 tablespoons chopped fresh parsley
- 3 tablespoons chopped fresh coriander
- Green side salad, to serve

DIRECTIONS

1. Clean and scale the fish. Cut it open lengthways from the head to the tail through the back. Rinse and pat dry with paper towels.

2. Place the fish under the grill for 5 minutes on each side until partially cooked, then transfer to an oven-proof dish.

3. In the meantime, heat the vegetable oil in a frying pan. Fry the onions and garlic, stirring occasionally until tender. Stir in the curry powder, dried lime, or lemon rind and salt.

4. Dissolve the tamarind paste in the warm water and add it to the onion mixture. Cook over a medium heat for 25 minutes, until it becomes a thick paste. Add the parsley and coriander.

5. Preheat the oven to 400°F. Spread the onion mixture over the grilled fish. Cook in the oven for 15–20 minutes until the fish is cooked.

6. Place the fish under the grill for 1 minute until a thin crust has formed on the stuffing.

7. Serve hot with a green salad.

BARBECUE
TAKES

This category is a fun one. The recipes featured in this section deserve their own moment for their inventiveness that will wow a crowd!

ATOMIC BUFFALO TURDS

BBQ PULLED PORK JALAPEÑO POPPERS

BBQ CHICKEN PIZZA

BBQ CHICKEN SALAD

SHEET PAN BBQ CHICKEN NACHOS

PORK BELLY PINWHEELS WITH ORANGE
MAPLE BOURBON GLAZE

SWEET AND SPICY BBQ MEATBALLS

THE BEST BBQ CHICKEN SALAD

ATOMIC BUFFALO TURDS

MAKES 32

PREP TIME: 1 HOUR | COOK TIME: 2 HOURS, 30 MINUTES

MIKE FANELLI | TELFORD, PENNSYLVANIA

Growing up, I used to get these at a local barbecue restaurant. Sadly, the restaurant went out of business, so I did my best to recreate these at home. These do take some time to make, but they're possibly the best dish that I make!

INGREDIENTS

- 16 jalapeños
- 1 pound thick cut bacon
- 8 ounces cream cheese
- One 12-ounce package smoked cocktail sausages (I used Hillshire Farm's Beef Lit'l Smokies)
- 1 teaspoon paprika
- 2 teaspoons your favorite rub
- Toothpicks

DIRECTIONS

1. Preheat smoker to 225°F.
2. Rinse and clean jalapeños.
3. Slice jalapeños in half, remove seeds, and set aside.
4. Cut bacon in half horizontally.
5. In a bowl, combine cream cheese and paprika. Mix until paprika is evenly spread through the cream cheese.
6. Spoon approximately a tablespoon of the cream cheese mixture into each jalapeño.
7. Place a sausage on top of cream cheese.
8. Wrap a half-slice of bacon around each jalapeño and sausage and secure with a toothpick.
9. Sprinkle a pinch of your favorite barbecue rub on top.
10. Place onto preheated smoker and cook for 2 hours and 30 minutes.
11. When they're done, remove from the smoker and pull out toothpicks.
12. Enjoy!

BBQ PULLED PORK JALAPEÑO POPPERS

SERVES 7+

PREP TIME: 1 HOUR, 45 MINUTES | COOK TIME: 45 MINUTES

LEO HUDSON | MESA, ARIZONA

I created this recipe for a 4th of July party. We were all told to bring appetizers, but I don't like to be basic. I wanted my dish to disappear before anyone else's. I had just smoked a large pulled pork with a homemade dry rub and a homemade barbecue sauce the day before, but I didn't want to just bring that. It would be too easy. I thought about tasty combinations that would not only be visual appealing, but also taste amazing. Jalapeño poppers are a staple with this group, so I decided to elevate each ingredient of the poppers to make them the best poppers anyone had ever had. Not only did I smoke the jalapeños before stuffing them, I added my homemade barbecue seasoning and barbecue sauce to the cream cheese. I laid the super tender pulled pork inside of the poppers, then wrapped them in double-smoked bacon. They looked great, but were still missing something, so I made a barbecue aioli and drizzled the poppers before serving. These babies were the life of the party. I set them out without tasting them myself and they disappeared, so I had to make another batch. And another . . . and so on. **Note: If your pulled pork was pre-made, these poppers only take about 30 minutes to make. If you're making the pulled pork for these poppers, it'll take about 6–8 hours, but the results are so worth it.**

INGREDIENTS

PULLED PORK:
- 2–3 pounds pork shoulder
- ½ cup brown sugar
- ¼ cup paprika
- 2 tablespoons chili powder
- 2 tablespoons garlic powder
- 2 tablespoons onion powder
- 2 teaspoons salt
- 2 teaspoons pepper
- 2 teaspoons cinnamon

BARBECUE SAUCE:
- Pinch of homemade barbecue rub (dry ingredients from above recipe)
- 1 cup ketchup

- ¾ cup apple cider vinegar
- 1 cup brown sugar
- 2 tablespoons mustard
- ½ cup apple cider

JALAPEÑO POPPERS:
- 4 large jalapeños
- 4 ounces cream cheese
- 2 tablespoons homemade barbecue sauce
- 8 strips bacon
- ½ cup leftover pulled pork

BARBECUE AIOLI:
- 2 tablespoons homemade barbecue sauce
- 1 tablespoon honey
- ¼ cup mayonnaise

DIRECTIONS

1. Make your pulled pork and rub first. Combine all of the spices listed and whisk until everything is well blended. Rub the pork shoulder with the seasonings and smoke at 225°F for 6–7 hours until it's fall-apart tender.

2. While the pork is cooking, make your barbecue sauce by combining all of the sauce ingredients in a saucepan and simmering over medium-low heat for 15 minutes until the sauce thickens. Remove from the burner and set aside.

3. Cut the jalapeños in half and remove the seeds. Heat the grill to 450–500°F and roast the jalapeños for 8 minutes until the skin is blistered. Remove and allow to cool. (You want the jalapeños to be cool before putting in the cream cheese so they don't melt.)

4. Combine the cream cheese with 2 tablespoons of barbecue sauce and a pinch of your barbecue spice. Stir until everything is well blended.

5. Once the jalapeños are cool, place a spoonful of the barbecue cream cheese in each jalapeño. Top the cream cheese with pulled pork. Wrap a strip of bacon around each popper and place in the smoker at 450°F for 18–20 minutes until the bacon crisps up. (You may need to increase temperature at the end to crisp the bacon.)

6. While the jalapeños are cooking, combine the honey, mayonnaise, and barbecue sauce in a bottle and shake to combine. Remove the poppers from the oven and drizzle with a little sweet barbecue aioli (or serve on the side) and serve immediately!

BBQ CHICKEN PIZZA

SERVES 4

PREP TIME: 15 MINUTES | COOK TIME: 30 MINUTES
SARA LUNDBERG | PORTLAND, OREGON

Inspired by my love for similar pizzas enjoyed at restaurants, I embarked on a mission to recreate this delectable delight at home, all while slashing the cost in half. Get ready to indulge in pure happiness!

INGREDIENTS

HOMEMADE BARBECUE SAUCE:
- 1 cup ketchup
- ¼ cup apple cider vinegar
- ¼ cup brown sugar
- 2 tablespoons molasses
- 1 tablespoon Worcestershire sauce
- 1 tablespoon yellow mustard
- 1 tablespoon chili powder
- Pinch cayenne pepper

PIZZA:
- 5 ounces boneless skinless chicken breasts, cut into strips
- 1 tablespoon olive oil
- 2 tablespoons of barbecue sauce (for chicken)
- Pizza crust, refrigerated (I used Pillsbury)
- 1 teaspoon cornmeal
- Homemade barbecue sauce (for drizzle, recipe below)
- 2 tablespoons shredded smoked Gouda cheese
- 2 cups shredded mozzarella cheese
- ¼ cup sliced red onion
- Fresh cilantro, chopped

DIRECTIONS

BARBECUE SAUCE:
1. Whisk all ingredients together.
2. Can store in fridge up to 2 weeks.

PIZZA:
1. Place chicken into a bowl with barbecue sauce. Mix and coat well.
2. Place oil into a skillet over medium heat. Once hot, add chicken and cook until no longer raw. Set aside.
3. Roll out pizza dough onto a cookie sheet lined with parchment paper.
4. Sprinkle cornmeal on uncooked pizza dough.
5. Bake the dough for the time indicated on the package (usually 7 minutes).
6. Time to make the pizza! Take dough out of the oven. Spread barbecue sauce on the pizza sprinkle the cheeses on top.
7. Sprinkle chicken and onions on top of the cheese.
8. Bake at 400°F for 10 minutes.
9. Finish off with cilantro and enjoy!

BARBECUE TAKES

BBQ CHICKEN SALAD

SERVES 4

COOK TIME: 15 MINUTES

SARA LUNDBERG | PORTLAND, OREGON

This recipe was passed down from my mom. Easy to make and so good! It's an original recipe with homemade barbecue sauce, crispy lettuce, and torilla strips on top.

INGREDIENTS

BARBECUE SAUCE:
- 1½ cups ketchup
- ¼ cup brown sugar
- 2 tablespoons apple cider vinegar
- 1 tablespoon Worcestershire sauce
- 1 tablespoon Dijon mustard
- 1 teaspoon smoked paprika
- ½ teaspoon garlic powder
- ½ teaspoon onion powder
- Salt and pepper, to taste

SALAD:
- 2 cups cooked and shredded chicken
- 4 cups chopped lettuce
- ½ cup corn
- ½ cup black beans, rinsed and drained
- ½ cup tortilla strips (optional, for garnish)
- Salt and pepper, to taste

DIRECTIONS

1. In a small saucepan, combine all the barbecue sauce ingredients over medium heat.
2. Stir well and bring the mixture to a simmer. Cook for 5–7 minutes, stirring occasionally, until the sauce thickens.
3. Remove from heat and let the barbecue sauce cool.
4. In a large bowl, combine the shredded chicken, lettuce, corn kernels, black beans.
5. Pour the cooled barbecue sauce over the salad. Season with salt and pepper to taste.
6. Divide the salad into individual serving bowls or plates.
7. Top each serving with tortilla strips for added crunch and presentation.

SHEET PAN BBQ CHICKEN NACHOS

SERVES 7+

PREP TIME: 15 MINUTES | COOK TIME: 45 MINUTES

SARA LUNDBERG | PORTLAND, OREGON

These mouthwatering nachos are a hit with my kids, and I adore how effortless they are to whip up. Get ready for a flavor-packed and family-friendly delight!

INGREDIENTS

- Tortilla chips (enough to cover a large baking sheet)
- 2 cups cooked and shredded chicken (seasoned with salt and pepper)
- 1 cup homemade barbecue sauce (ingredients below)
- 1 cup shredded cheddar cheese
- ½ cup diced bell peppers (any color)
- ¼ cup sliced jalapeños (optional)
- ¼ cup chopped fresh cilantro
- Handful shredded lettuce
- 1 Roma tomato, chopped
- Sour cream, guacamole, and salsa for serving (store-bought)

BARBECUE SAUCE:
- 1 cup ketchup
- ¼ cup brown sugar
- ¼ cup apple cider vinegar
- 2 tablespoons Worcestershire sauce
- 2 tablespoons molasses
- 1 tablespoon Dijon mustard
- 1 teaspoon garlic powder
- 1 teaspoon onion powder
- ½ teaspoon smoked paprika
- Salt and pepper, to taste

DIRECTIONS

1. Preheat oven to 375°F and line a large baking sheet with parchment paper or aluminum foil.

2. Spread the tortilla chips in a single layer on the prepared baking sheet.

3. In a small saucepan, combine all the barbecue sauce ingredients. Cook over medium heat, stirring occasionally, until the sauce thickens and the flavors meld together. Remove from heat.

4. Mix the cooked and shredded chicken with 1 cup of the homemade barbecue sauce until well coated.

5. Spread the barbecue chicken evenly over the tortilla chips.

6. Sprinkle the shredded cheddar cheese over the chicken and chips.

7. Distribute the diced bell peppers, diced tomatoes, and sliced jalapeños (if using) over the top.

8. Place the baking sheet in the preheated oven and bake for about 10–12 minutes or until the cheese is melted and bubbly.

9. Remove the sheet pan from the oven and let it cool for a minute.

10. Sprinkle the shredded lettuce and chopped cilantro over the nachos for a burst of freshness.

11. Serve the sheet pan nachos hot with sour cream, guacamole, and salsa on the side.

PORK BELLY PINWHEELS

SERVES 6

WITH ORANGE MAPLE BOURBON GLAZE

PREP TIME: 30 MINUTES | COOK TIME: 5 HOURS
JORDAN HANGER | BARTOW, FLORIDA

There's nothing more decadent and delicious than smoked pork belly. In my opinion, it's one of the best things to smoke low and slow. The recipe is fairly simple, and the glaze only has four ingredients. It makes for a delicious appetizer and is always a crowd favorite. The sweet and savory glaze really compliments the pork and turns it into meat candy! I mean, who wouldn't want that? Check out more of my barbecue recipes on TheNinjaCue.com.

INGREDIENTS

- 1 slab pork belly cut into strips (3-4 pounds)
- 4 tablespoons all-purpose barbecue seasoning

ORANGE MAPLE BOURBON GLAZE:

- ½ cup fresh orange juice
- ¼ cup brown sugar
- ¼ cup bourbon
- ¼ cup brown sugar

DIRECTIONS

1. Start by cutting 1-inch strips of pork belly. Remove skin if on.

2. Season with your favorite barbecue rub, then roll into a pinwheel.

3. Take a skewer and push it through the meat.

4. Smoke at 250°F for about 3 hours.

5. In the meantime, make a glaze using fresh orange juice, maple syrup, bourbon, and brown sugar. Whisk over medium-low heat and reduce until it thickens. As it cools down, it will get thicker.

6. Brush the glaze onto your pork belly a few times and smoke for up to 2 more hours, or until the internal temperature reaches 200°F and the pork belly is bite-through tender.

7. Brush on glaze one more time just before serving. Enjoy!

> ## "BARBECUE IS THE GREAT EQUALIZER. IT BRINGS PEOPLE TOGETHER."
>
> **—MYRON MIXON, BBQ CHEF, PIT MASTER, AND AUTHOR**

SWEET AND SPICY BBQ MEATBALLS

SERVES 4

PREP TIME: 45 MINUTES | COOK TIME: 30 MINUTES

RAY SHEEHAN | NEW EGYPT, NEW JERSEY

These barbecue meatballs are packed with flavor. They're easy to assemble and come together quickly, so they're great for entertaining or a weeknight meal. We make these a lot for tailgating.

INGREDIENTS

SWEET AND SPICY BARBECUE SAUCE:
- 1¼ cups ketchup
- 1 cup light brown sugar, packed
- ¼ cup molasses
- ¼ cup apple cider vinegar
- ¼ cup water
- 1 tablespoon Worcestershire sauce
- 2 tablespoons prepared mustard
- 2 teaspoons smoked paprika
- ½ teaspoon granulated garlic
- 1 teaspoon freshly ground black pepper
- ½ teaspoon cayenne pepper

MEATBALLS:
- 1½ pounds meatloaf mix (beef, pork, veal blend)
- ¾ cup seasoned breadcrumbs
- ⅓ cup parmesan cheese
- 2 eggs
- 1 teaspoon Worcestershire sauce
- 1 tablespoon fresh parsley chopped
- 2 cloves garlic, minced
- 1 teaspoon Italian seasoning
- 1 small onion, finely chopped
- Salt, to taste
- Freshly ground pepper, to taste

DIRECTIONS

SWEET AND SPICY BARBECUE SAUCE:

1. In a medium-sized saucepan, combine all the sauce ingredients and bring to a gentle boil over medium heat, stirring to dissolve the sugar.

2. Lower the heat to low and simmer until slightly thickened, 5–6 minutes, stirring occasionally.

3. Keep the sauce warm until you're ready to use it. Store leftover sauce in a jar in the refrigerator for up to a month.

MEATBALLS:

1. Prepare a charcoal grill to cook at 375°F and set up for two-zone cooking. Light a charcoal chimney, and when the edges of the charcoal at the top of the chimney begin to ash over, dump the pile of hot coals onto one side of the grill to form your hot side (direct cooking), leaving the other side empty to form your cool side (indirect cooking), forming 2 zones.

2. In a large bowl combine the ground meats, breadcrumbs, parmesan cheese, eggs, Worcestershire sauce, parsley, garlic, Italian seasoning, onion, and salt and pepper to taste.

3. Form the meat into golf ball-sized balls, about 2 ounces each.

4. Once your grill reaches temperature, place the meatballs, seam side down, on the cooking grate over the indirect heat zone with the grill lid on.

5. After about 20 minutes, glaze the meatballs with the barbecue sauce and place them back on the cooker for another 10 minutes, or until the meatballs reach an internal temperature of 160°F.

6. Remove the meatballs from the grill and allow them to rest for 5 minutes before serving.

THE BEST BBQ CHICKEN SALAD

SERVES 4

PREP TIME: 15 MINUTES | COOK TIME: 15 MINUTES

SARA LUNDBERG | PORTLAND, OREGON

My best friend's barbecue chicken salad is a warm-weather delight. With tender grilled chicken, crisp greens, tangy barbecue sauce, and a medley of colorful veggies, it's a family favorite that even my kids can't resist. It's the perfect balance of flavors and textures.

INGREDIENTS

BARBECUE SAUCE:
- ¼ cup water
- 2 cups ketchup
- 5 tablespoons dark brown sugar
- 5 tablespoons sugar
- 1 tablespoon mustard powder
- 2 tablespoons lemon juice
- 5 tablespoons apple cider vinegar
- 2 tablespoons Worchester sauce

SALAD:
- One 12-ounce package of lettuce mix
- ½ cup black beans, rinsed and drained
- 1 cup corn
- 1 teaspoon cilantro, finely chopped
- 2 tablespoons diced tomatoes
- ½ cup your favorite shredded cheese
- 1 cup cooked and shredded chicken
- ¼ cup ranch dressing
- ¼ cup barbecue sauce (see recipe)

DIRECTIONS

BARBECUE SAUCE:
1. Mix all the ingredients together.
2. You can keep the barbecue in the fridge for up to 2 weeks.

SALAD:
1. Combine the ranch dressing and barbecue sauce together.
2. Combine barbecue ranch with all other ingredients in a large bowl.
3. Enjoy!

SIDES

While barbecue is the star of the show, your plate won't be complete without some seriously good side dishes. There's a little bit of everything here, so you can pick and choose and change it up every cookout!

BBQ PINEAPPLE 🥕

BEER CHEESE MAC AND CHEESE 🥕

CAMPFIRE BEANS

COUNTRY CORNBREAD 🥕

DEVILED EGGS 🥕

ELOTE (GRILLED MEXICAN CORN) 🥕

GRILLED CORN MAQUE CHOUX WITH CHARRED LEMON VINAIGRETTE

GRILLED VEGETABLE CHILI RELLENOS 🥕

GRILLED VEGGIE SKEWERS 🥕

HOMEMADE CHIPS 🥕

JACK'S BEANS 🥕

LOADED POTATO SALAD

SMOKED BAKED BEANS

SMOKED GREEN BEANS

SWEET AND SPICY BACON WRAPPED BBQ CARROTS

🥕 *Recipes with this symbol represent a vegetarian dish.*

BBQ PINEAPPLE

PREP TIME: 15 MINUTES | COOK TIME: 15 MINUTES

SARA LUNDBERG | PORTLAND, OREGON

During my pregnancy with twins, I discovered this delightful barbecue pineapple recipe that satisfied one of my strongest cravings.

INGREDIENTS

- 1 pineapple, cut into cubes or rings
- 2 tablespoons butter
- 1 cup barbecue sauce (see recipe)

BARBECUE SAUCE:

- 1 cup ketchup
- ¼ cup brown sugar
- ¼ cup apple cider vinegar
- 2 tablespoons Worcestershire sauce
- 1 tablespoon Dijon mustard
- 1 teaspoon garlic powder
- 1 teaspoon onion powder
- ½ teaspoon smoked paprika
- Salt and pepper, to taste

DIRECTIONS

1. Combine the ketchup, brown sugar, apple cider vinegar, Worcestershire sauce, Dijon mustard, garlic powder, onion powder, smoked paprika, salt, and pepper. Whisk the ingredients together until well combined.

2. Place mixture in a saucepan over medium heat and bring to a simmer.

3. Reduce the heat to low and let the sauce simmer for about 10–15 minutes, stirring occasionally.

4. Taste the sauce and adjust the seasonings according to your preference.

5. Remove the sauce from heat and let it cool before using.

6. Once cooled, generously brush the butter then the barbecue sauce over pineapple slices.

7. Grill the pineapple slices on a preheated grill or stovetop grill pan for about 3–4 minutes per side, or until nicely caramelized and grill marks appear.

8. Serve the barbecue pineapple slices as a delightful side dish or as a topping for burgers, sandwiches, or salads.

BEER CHEESE MAC AND CHEESE

SERVES 8

COOK TIME: 30 MINUTES

KIM WILCOX | KNOXVILLE, TENNESSEE

This Beer Cheese Mac and Cheese is rich and bold dish—heaven in a bowl. For a real treat, serve this with warm soft pretzels. Use pasta shapes that have nooks and crannies that will "trap" the cheese. Anything with ridges, hollow centers, or corkscrews will hang on to that cheesy goodness. Some of the best cheeses to use for mac and cheese are those that melt well, such as sharp cheddar, Gruyère, cream cheese, gouda, and the extra-tangy goat cheese. If you can find sharp cheddar with peppers in it, you can make a great sauce. The darker the beer you use in this recipe, the more beer flavor your sauce will have. This recipe is perfect for trying endless possibilities based on your preferences!

INGREDIENTS

VEGETARIAN

- 16 ounces rigatoni pasta
- 4 tablespoons butter
- 6 tablespoons flour
- 2 cups whole milk
- 1 cup beer of your choice
- 1 teaspoon salt
- ½ teaspoon pepper
- ½ teaspoon paprika
- ½ teaspoon garlic
- ½ teaspoon dried mustard
- 2 cups shredded sharp cheddar
- 1 cup shredded Gruyère
- Green onions and chili pepper blend or red pepper flakes, for garnish (optional)

DIRECTIONS

1. Cook the pasta according to the package directions, drain and set aside.

2. Make a roux by putting the butter and flour in a medium pot and cooking on medium heat until the butter melts and the mixture starts to bubble, making sure to whisk to avoid burning. Cook for 1 minute.

3. Slowly whisk in the milk, then add the beer and whisk. Let the mixture come to a simmer.

4. Add the salt, pepper, paprika, garlic, and dried mustard, then mix well. Remove from the heat and set aside.

5. Slowly add the shredded cheese and stir until it melts and is creamy.

6. Add the pasta and mix well.

7. If desired, garnish with green onion and chili pepper blend or red pepper flakes.

8. Serve hot and enjoy!

SIDES

CAMPFIRE BEANS

SERVES 7+

PREP TIME: 30 MINUTES | COOK TIME: 1 HOUR

JENNINE | BLAINE, MINNESOTA

My grandparents put their own spin on a recipe they found in a small-town cookbook!

INGREDIENTS

- ⅓ cup brown sugar, packed
- ½ cup ketchup
- 1 teaspoon dry mustard
- ½ cup barbecue sauce
- ⅓ cup sugar
- ½ teaspoon chili powder
- ½ teaspoon salt
- ¼ teaspoon pepper
- ½ pound ground beef, browned and drained
- ½ pound bacon, cooked, drained, and crumbled
- ½ pound bratwurst, cut into 1-inch slices, cooked, and drained
- Two 15-ounce cans kidney beans, rinsed and drained
- One 16-ounce can pork and beans
- One 15-ounce can chili pinto beans in sauce

DIRECTIONS

1. In a large mixing bowl, combine first 8 ingredients and mix well.
2. Stir in meat and beans.
3. Pour into a 2-quart casserole dish and bake at 350°F uncovered for 1 hour or until heated through.

HOT TIP

Alternatively, you can also heat in crockpot on low for 1 hour or until heated through.

SIDES

COUNTRY CORNBREAD

COOK TIME: 30 MINUTES

KIM WILCOX | KNOXVILLE, TENNESSEE

My family loves cornbread and we tend to enjoy it a little on the sweet side, which is not always a popular opinion. You can use this recipe and omit the sugar if your family gravitates more toward savory. Either way, it's a delightfully flavorful and moist cornbread. This cornbread is great topped with butter, honey, honey butter, or jam. For a nice flavor variation, substitute a small can of chopped green chilies for the corn. For a real treat, put a few tablespoons of pimento cheese on top of the bread and broil it for a few minutes until the cheese is soft and melting.

INGREDIENTS

- 2½ cups self-rising yellow cornmeal
- 2 cups buttermilk
- ⅓ cup melted shortening (I used Crisco)
- 2 eggs, beaten
- ¼ cup sugar
- 1½ teaspoons kosher salt
- One 15¼-ounce can corn, partially drained

DIRECTIONS

1. Preheat the oven to 350°F.
2. Grease a 9x13 pan, use cupcake liners in a cupcake pan, or lightly grease a cast iron skillet.
3. Mix all the ingredients together in a bowl and stir gently to incorporate.
4. Bake for 20–25 minutes or until golden brown. Serve hot.

DEVILED EGGS

SERVES 8–12

PREP TIME: 20 MINUTES | COOK TIME: 20 MINUTES
KIM WILCOX | KNOXVILLE, TENNESSEE

You can't go wrong with a side of deviled eggs! As a helpful trick to make the task of peeling the eggs easier, place the eggs in a bowl of ice cold water after boiling. After about 10–15 minutes, lightly tap the eggs on a cutting board or hard surface to make them crack, roll back and forth under your hand, then carefully peel off the shell.

INGREDIENTS

- 12 eggs
- ⅓ cup mayonnaise
- 1½ tablespoons yellow mustard
- ½ teaspoon sugar
- ⅛ teaspoon fine ground pepper
- ¼ teaspoon salt
- 1 tablespoon apple cider vinegar
- ½–1 teaspoon paprika or similar seasoning, for garnish (I used Old Bay seasoning)

DIRECTIONS

1. Hard boil and peel a dozen eggs. Slice each in half lengthwise, remove the yolks, and place them in a small bowl. Arrange the egg whites on a tray or platter.

2. Use a fork, food processor, or handheld mixer to mash the yolks. Add the remaining ingredients to the yolks and mix until smooth. Adjust the seasoning to your liking.

3. Top each egg white half with some filling. You can use a spoon, but it helps to use a pastry bag to pipe the filling into the eggs so that they look pretty.

4. Finish with a sprinkle of Old Bay seasoning, paprika, or similar.

"BARBECUE IS A CELEBRATION OF CULTURE, A CELEBRATION OF TRADITION, A CELEBRATION OF PEOPLE."

—RODNEY SCOTT, CHEF AND PITMASTER

SIDES

GRILLED CORN MAQUE CHOUX

SERVES 4

WITH CHARRED LEMON VINAIGRETTE

PREP TIME: 30 MINUTES | COOK TIME: 1 HOUR

NATE FIGARO | KNIGHTDALE, NORTH CAROLINA

This is a dish my mom and her mom would make on Sunday afternoons as a side dish. My mom would use her dad's cast-iron Dutch oven to cook it in. I wanted to add my own twist, so I added bacon and grilled lemons to create a smoky vinaigrette. It has a great balance of smokiness from the corn and bell peppers with the saltiness of the bacon, and the sweet, acidic flavor from the grilled lemon vinaigrette.

INGREDIENTS

GRILLED CORN MAQUE CHOUX:

- 3 slices bacon, diced
- 8 whole ears of corn
- 2 tablespoons butter, unsalted
- 1 red bell pepper
- 5 cherry tomatoes, diced
- 4 cloves garlic, minced
- 3 tablespoons smoky Creole barbecue rub

CHARRED LEMON VINAIGRETTE:

- 4 strips bacon
- Smoky Creole barbecue rub, to taste
- 2 tablespoons of Dijon mustard
- ¼ cup red wine vinegar
- Juice from 1 whole lemon
- ½ cup extra virgin olive oil
- 1 teaspoon oregano
- ¼ teaspoon black pepper
- 1 tablespoon hot honey

DIRECTIONS

GRILLED CORN MAQUE CHOUX:

1. Remove husk from corn and run under cold water.
2. Light half a charcoal chimney with briquettes. Wait for all briquettes to turn gray, about 10–15 minutes.
3. Bank charcoal to one side of grill (making a hot zone and a cool zone).
4. Add 2–3 chunks of mesquite wood to coals.
5. Place bell pepper over coal and rotate until pepper is fully charred on all sides. Then set aside in a resealable plastic bag. (Steam from the pepper will make removing the charred skin easier.) Once cooled, dice bell pepper.
6. Place corn over coals for 10–15 minutes, or until corn begins to char.
7. Remove corn from grill and set aside.
8. Set sauté pan to medium heat and add unsalted butter.
9. Add minced garlic, diced bell pepper, diced bacon, and corn.
10. Season with smoky Creole barbecue rub.
11. Place corn maque choux on plate and add sliced tomatoes and Charred Lemon Vinaigrette.

CHARRED LEMON VINAIGRETTE:

1. Set oven to 375°F.
2. Place four strips of bacon on baking pan and season with Creole barbecue rub.
3. Place bacon in oven at 375°F for 12–15 minutes.
4. Pour Dijon mustard, red wine vinegar, and lemon juice into bowl and begin to whisk.
5. Slowly add hot honey and extra virgin olive oil to bowl and continue to whisk.
6. Add oregano and black pepper.

ELOTE
(GRILLED MEXICAN CORN)

SERVES 4

PREP TIME: 15 MINUTES | COOK TIME: 15 MINUTES

TRACI ANTONOVICH | SONOMA COUNTY, CALIFORNIA

This easy Mexican corn recipe was born from my need to enjoy street corn on demand. It's my homemade interpretation of the Mexican street corn from my local street fair vendor. Everyone does street corn differently, but here, corn on the cob is grilled, cream sauce-slathered, topped with Cotija cheese, and irresistibly seasoned. The best part is nobody turns down street corn at a barbecue!

INGREDIENTS

VEGETARIAN

- **4 ears corn on the cob**
- **Oil, as needed**
- **¼ cup mayonnaise**
- **¼ cup sour cream or Mexican crema**
- **1 lime, zested and juiced**
- **½ cup crumbled Cotija cheese**
- **Chili powder or similar seasoning (I used Tajín seasoning)**
- **Fresh cilantro, optional for garnish**

DIRECTIONS

1. Preheat grill to medium-high, or to a temperature of 350°F. Brush grates to clean, then lightly coat with oil.

2. Remove husks and silk from corn, then rinse and pat dry to remove excess moisture.

3. Brush a light coating of oil over corn. Set corn on the preheated grill, close lid, and grill 4 to 5 minutes on each side, or until kernels are tender and slightly charred.

4. Meanwhile, combine mayonnaise, sour cream, lime zest, and lime juice in mixing bowl.

5. Transfer corn off the grill and brush the creamy mixture over the entire surface.

6. Sprinkle a layer of Cotija cheese to cover the corn surface, followed by a sprinkle of chili seasoning.

7. Serve immediately with optional cilantro garnish.

SIDES

GRILLED VEGETABLE CHILI RELLENOS

SERVES 6

PREP TIME: 45 MINUTES | COOK TIME: 15 MINUTES

RAY SHEEHAN | NEW EGYPT, NEW JERSEY

I won first place with this recipe in a competition that my local farmer's market was hosting. You can add or subtract various vegetables according to your preference. These are great for tailgating or for #meatlessmondays.

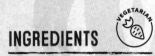

INGREDIENTS

- 6 poblano chilies
- 1 tablespoon olive oil
- 1 small red onion, finely chopped
- 4 garlic cloves, minced
- 1½ cups corn kernels cut from 2 grilled cobs
- One 15-ounce can fire-roasted diced tomatoes, drained
- One 15-ounce can black beans, drained and rinsed
- 2 tablespoons cilantro, chopped
- 1 teaspoon dried cumin
- ½ teaspoon dried oregano
- 1 tablespoon fresh lime juice
- 1½ cups shredded Asadero or Colby Jack cheese
- Kosher salt, to taste
- Ground black pepper, to taste

DIRECTIONS

1. Set up a charcoal grill for two-zone cooking. Light a charcoal chimney, and when the edges of the charcoal at the top of the chimney begin to ash over, dump the pile of hot coals onto one side of the grill to form your hot side (direct cooking), leaving the other side empty to make your cool side (indirect cooking), forming 2 zones.

2. When the cooker is ready, grill the poblanos, turning frequently, until softened and charred on all sides, about 12–15 minutes.

3. Remove peppers from the grill and place them in a bowl covered with plastic wrap. Let stand until cool enough to handle.

4. Peel the charred skins off the peppers, then split them lengthwise and remove seeds. This is easier to do under running water.

5. Pat the peppers dry and set aside.

6. Heat the olive oil in a large skillet over medium heat and sauté the onion and garlic for 3–5 minutes until tender.

7. Remove from heat and stir in the corn, tomatoes, beans, cilantro, salt, pepper, cumin, oregano, lime juice, and half of the cheese.

8. Stuff peppers with the corn and bean mixture, and top with the remaining cheese.

9. Arrange the peppers on the indirect heat side of the grill. Close the lid and cook until the cheese melts and the filling is hot, about 5–7 minutes.

10. Remove from the grill and arrange on a platter to serve.

SIDES

GRILLED VEGGIE SKEWERS

SERVES 6

PREP TIME: 15 MINUTES | COOK TIME: 20 MINUTES

BRIANNE GRAJKOWSKI | SAN DIEGO, CALIFORNIA

It's not a proper cookout or barbecue without a veggie skewer on the side! Super simple and easy to customize, this recipe is a great summertime staple when feeding a crowd.

INGREDIENTS

- 1 red bell pepper
- 1 yellow bell pepper
- 1 green bell pepper
- 1 cup mushrooms
- ½ cup cherry tomatoes
- 1 tablespoon olive oil
- 1 teaspoon salt

DIRECTIONS

1. Slice peppers down the sides, around the core. Slice into 1-inch chunks.
2. Use a paper towel to clean off mushroom tops. Pull mushroom stems off and discard. Slice mushroom tops in half.
3. Add veggies to bamboo skewers, alternating colors and veggies. Repeat until all veggies are used up.
4. Brush on olive oil and sprinkle with salt.
5. Grill at 350°F for 12 to 15 minutes, rotating every few minutes.

SIDES

HOMEMADE CHIPS

SERVES 4

PREP TIME: 30 MINUTES | COOK TIME: 15 MINUTES
KIM WILCOX | KNOXVILLE, TENNESSEE

Making homemade potato chips is so underrated, yet so easy! All you need are a few ingredients and I guarantee you'll prefer these over any store-bought chips. It also helps if you have a mandolin to slice the potatoes as thinly and as easily as possible—just be careful!

INGREDIENTS

VEGETARIAN

- 3–4 potatoes, washed and unpeeled
- 3–4 sweet potatoes, washed and unpeeled
- Seasoning of choice, for garnish (I used salt and Trader Joe's® Everything But the Elote Seasoning Blend)
- Oil, for cooking

DIRECTIONS

1. Slice the potatoes very thinly and soak them in an ice-water bath for about 20–30 minutes.

2. Drain the potatoes, lay them on paper towels, and pat completely dry.

3. Heat the oil in a heavy skillet to 375°F. It is important that the oil is hot before you put the potato slices into it so that the chips don't soak up the oil before they begin frying.

4. Carefully place the potato slices in the hot oil and fry until they are a light golden brown.

5. Remove them with a slotted spoon and place them on paper towels to drain the excess oil off.

6. Season while warm.

JACK'S BEANS

SERVES 7+

PREP TIME: 20 MINUTES | COOK TIME: 60–90 MINUTES

KIM WILCOX | KNOXVILLE, TENNESSEE

There's nothing better than a great pot of baked beans at a barbecue. It's always first up on my plate. When making these, I have always used more than one type of bean because it adds texture, flavor, and visual appeal. In this recipe I used pinto, black, dark red kidney, chili, and light red beans. Also, the better the Jack, the better the beans!

INGREDIENTS

VEGETARIAN

BEANS:

- Five 15½-ounce cans beans
- 2 cups hickory smoked barbecue sauce
- ⅔ cup whiskey (I used Jack Daniels)
- 1 teaspoon salt
- Dash of pepper

TOPPING:

- ⅓ cup brown sugar
- 1 teaspoon jerk seasoning
  (I used Olde Virden's Tennessee
  Jerk Seasoning)

DIRECTIONS

1. Preheat oven to 350°F.

2. Drain the beans in a colander.

3. When drained, put in a medium mixing bowl and add barbecue sauce, whiskey, salt, and pepper.

4. Stir well and place in a casserole or other dish and bake at 350°F until bubbly and sauce has thickened.

5. In a small bowl, mix the brown sugar and jerk seasoning well and sprinkle on top of the beans.

6. Caramelize under the broiler or with a kitchen torch. Let sit for a few minutes until the sugar hardens.

7. Serve!

SIDES

LOADED POTATO SALAD

SERVES 7+

PREP TIME: 15 MINUTES | COOK TIME: 15 MINUTES
TRACI ANTONOVICH | SONOMA COUNTY, CALIFORNIA

Not everyone loves potato salad (crazy, I know!), but everyone loves loaded baked potatoes, which is exactly why I created this recipe. A bowl of loaded potatoes is the best of both worlds, especially because it has bacon, cheddar, and onions in a mouthwatering sour cream dressing. I wanted a quick and easy potato salad that would complement any grilled or smoked meat at any gathering and would get devoured. This one always ends up as an empty bowl, which always speaks for itself! **Note: While this recipe does include bacon, simply omit for a vegetarian alternative!**

INGREDIENTS

- 3 pounds russet potatoes, 1-inch diced
- 1½ cups sour cream
- ½ cup mayonnaise
- 1 tablespoon white vinegar
- 1 teaspoon sea salt
- ½ teaspoon black pepper
- 8 slices bacon, cooked and crumbled
- 2 green onions, thinly sliced
- 4 ounces shredded cheddar cheese

DIRECTIONS

1. Carefully place diced potatoes in 3 quarts boiling water for 10–15 minutes until they are fork-tender. Alternatively, you can use any method to cook the potatoes.

2. Drain potatoes and cool to room temperature.

3. In a small mixing bowl, whisk together sour cream, mayonnaise, vinegar, salt, and pepper.

4. Place potatoes, bacon, green onions, and cheddar cheese in a large mixing bowl.

5. Pour dressing mixture over potatoes, and gently toss to coat.

6. Serve warm or chilled.

HOT TIP

To store, cool completely and refrigerate up to five days in an airtight container.

SIDES

SMOKED BAKED BEANS

SERVES 7+

PREP TIME: 15 MINUTES | COOK TIME: 1 HOUR

DUSTIN SHERIN | SPERRY, OKLAHOMA

My wife's grandmother made some of the best baked beans I had ever had, ten out of ten. She gave me the recipe and I turned it up to 11 by cooking it on the Hasty Bake and making it super smoky. I don't make barbecue without them. It's super easy and takes about an hour after your main course is patiently resting and getting ready to serve.

INGREDIENTS

- One 117-ounce can baked beans, drained (I used Bush's Original Baked Beans)
- 1 sweet onion
- 1 red bell pepper
- 7 ounces kielbasa sausage
- Favorite barbecue rub/seasoning
- Salt
- Pepper

DIRECTIONS

1. Chop sweet onion and dice red bell pepper.
2. Put half of the onion and red bell pepper in 11x14 aluminum pan
3. Dump half of the can of baked beans in pan.
4. Add remaining onion and red bell pepper, followed by the remaining beans.
5. Mix thoroughly.
6. Once combined, slice kielbasa in ⅛-inch-thick slices, then halve the slices.
7. Place slices to cover entire top surface of beans.
8. Season with salt, pepper, and your preferred barbecue seasoning or dry rub all over the top of kielbasa.
9. Place on smoker uncovered at approximately 325°F–350°F with heavy apple wood smoke for approximately 30 minutes.
10. Mix contents.
11. Cover and cook another 30 minutes or until warm.
12. Serve and enjoy!

HOT TIP

You can add sriracha for an extra kick.

SIDES

SMOKED GREEN BEANS

SERVES 7+

PREP TIME: 15 MINUTES | COOK TIME: 3 HOURS
CAREY BRINGLE | NASHVILLE, TENNESSEE

We have used this recipe to compete in barbecue competitions for 30+ years and have served it in one of our restaurants, Peg Leg Porker, since we opened 10 years ago. It is one of our top selling sides and is the one we get asked for the recipe for the most, almost daily. It's a family and customer favorite! **Note: If looking to make the dish vegetarian, you can prepare this recipe the exact same way, just without the bacon.**

INGREDIENTS

- 6 cups green beans, trimmed and chopped into 1-inch pieces
- 2 cups water
- 2 tablespoons apple cider vinegar
- ¼ white onion, cut into slivers
- ¼ pounds bacon, diced
- 2 teaspoons pepper, or to taste
- 1 teaspoon salt, or to taste

DIRECTIONS

1. Preheat your grill or smoker to 250°F.
2. In large cast-iron skillet or casserole dish, place all ingredients.
3. Place dish or skillet in smoker, uncovered.
4. Smoke for 3 hours, stirring hourly.
5. Remove from the smoker and serve hot.

SWEET AND SPICY BACON WRAPPED BBQ CARROTS

SERVES 6

PREP TIME: 15 MINUTES | COOK TIME: 45 MINUTES

RAY SHEEHAN | NEW EGYPT, NEW JERSEY

I started making these because my wife said we needed to serve more vegetables at our cookouts!

INGREDIENTS

- ⅓ cup real maple syrup
- 1 tablespoon sriracha sauce
- 2 pounds carrots, 1-inch thick and well-scrubbed or peeled
- 1 pound classic thin cut bacon
- 1 teaspoon freshly ground black pepper
- ½ teaspoon garlic powder
- 2 teaspoons chopped fresh parsley

DIRECTIONS

1. Prepare a charcoal grill for indirect cooking, about 400°F. Light a charcoal chimney, and when the edges of the charcoal at the top of the chimney begin to ash over, dump the pile of hot coals onto one side of the grill to form your hot side (direct cooking), leaving the other side empty to form your cool side (indirect cooking) forming 2 zones.

2. Line a sheet pan with aluminum foil, spray a baking rack with nonstick spray, and place the rack on top of the foil.

3. In a small bowl, combine the maple syrup and sriracha sauce. Set aside.

4. Prepare the carrots. Wrap each carrot with a slice of bacon and place them on the prepared baking sheet.

5. Dust the carrots with the black pepper and garlic powder to season.

6. Once the grill comes up to temperature, place the tray with the carrots on the indirect side of the grill and close the lid. Cook for about 25 minutes. Then, using tongs, carefully turn the carrots over and baste with the maple sriracha sauce. Close the lid and continue cooking, turning occasionally, for another 20–25 minutes (depending on the thickness of the carrots) or until the carrots are cooked through and the bacon is crisp.

7. Remove the carrots from the grill and baste them with any remaining sauce.

8. Sprinkle with chopped parsley and serve immediately.

SAUCES, RUBS, AND MARINADES

Arguably the most fun aspect of barbecue is concocting sauces, rubs, and marinades. You can get so creative and combine so many ingredients, all depending on what you'd like to achieve. While some of the best rubs are simple, others burst with flavor.

AUTHENTIC JAMAICAN JERK CHICKEN MARINADE

AWARD-WINNING BBQ SAUCE

CAROLINA VINEGAR BBQ SAUCE

DUDE'S DYNAMITE BBQ SAUCE

GOOT OLE BBQ BEEF MARINADE

GOOT OLE BBQ TURKEY BRINE

SAN FRANCISCO BBQ SAUCE

SAVORY SWEET DRY RUB FOR RIBS

TRACI'S HOMEMADE BBQ SAUCE

AUTHENTIC JAMAICAN JERK CHICKEN MARINADE

YIELDS 6-8 CUPS

PREP TIME: 6+ HOURS | COOK TIME: 1 HOUR, 30 MINUTES

ACHUNCHIGAN LATTORE | ORMOND BEACH, FLORIDA

Being a native Jamaican, I had to learn how to make my own jerk marinade. Over the last few years, my recipe has been refined to fit my family's preferences. Since I also invite guests over quite often, I do take this into consideration. One of the biggest concerns about jerk marinades is the tendency to be spicy because of the Scotch bonnet pepper. However, what I have figured out is how to tame the spice or let it loose, based on who you're trying to cater for. These days, I either remove seeds and membranes, or reduce the number of peppers in the recipe. That has helped to make this recipe a crowd favorite at any backyard barbecue. **Note: This exact recipe is a mild jerk marinade and not spicy. Even if you taste it fresh and you get a good spicy bite, have no fear. Once cooked, the spice will mellow out into a great refreshing and flavorful jerk bite.**

INGREDIENTS

- 1 yellow onion, diced
- 1 bunch of green onions, diced
- 1 bulb garlic, minced
- 1 thumb of ginger, minced
- 1 bunch of fresh thyme, chopped
- ½ teaspoon nutmeg
- 1 teaspoon ground allspice
- ½ teaspoon cinnamon
- 3–4 tablespoons kosher salt
- 2 tablespoons white vinegar
- 2 tablespoons vegetable oil
- 1 tablespoon whole allspice (pimento) berries
- 2 fresh oranges, squeezed OR ½ cup orange juice
- 1–2 teaspoons browning or molasses, for color
- 5 Scotch bonnet peppers (2 green, 3 ripe)

DIRECTIONS

1. Leave green Scotch bonnet peppers whole and remove seeds from ripened peppers for a mild marinade. Leave all seeds and membranes in for more spice. Add more salt if you want it saltier.

2. Blend all the ingredients in a food processor or a blender. If you want less liquid, reduce the oil and vinegar amounts.

3. Place the chicken in marinade overnight or for about 12–24 hours (4–6 tablespoons per pound).

4. Be sure to rub some of the marinade under the skin of the chicken as well. When it comes time to cook, prepare meat in an oven, grill, or a smoker. Cook between 300–350°F until the breast temperature reaches 165°F internally. If you decide to use a smoker, using wood like oak, cherry, pecan, hickory, or apple are all suitable. If you use a bold smoke flavor like mesquite, you could get close to the robust smoke flavor of pimento wood.

Note: To save the remaining marinade, store in the refrigerator for up to 3 months.

AWARD-WINNING BBQ SAUCE

SERVES 6

PREP TIME: 15 MINUTES | COOK TIME: 15 MINUTES
SARA LUNDBERG | PORTLAND, OREGON

Get ready to taste the magic of an award-winning barbecue sauce recipe! Unearthed from an antique store's hidden treasure—a charming recipe box—it proudly boasts a blue ribbon from the local fair.

INGREDIENTS

- ¼ cup water
- 2 cups ketchup
- 5 tablespoons dark brown sugar
- 5 tablespoons sugar
- 1 tablespoon mustard powder
- 2 tablespoons lemon juice
- 5 tablespoons apple cider vinegar
- 2 tablespoons Worcestershire sauce

DIRECTIONS

1. Mix all the ingredients together.
2. Enjoy!

Note: You can keep this barbecue sauce in the fridge for up to 2 weeks.

CAROLINA VINEGAR BBQ SAUCE

SERVES 7+

PREP TIME: 15 MINUTES | COOK TIME: 15 MINUTES

MIKE HULTQUIST | HUNTERSVILLE, NORTH CAROLINA

I learned how to make this simple Carolina Vinegar BBQ Sauce shortly after I moved to North Carolina. It is essential for pulled pork!

INGREDIENTS

FOR EASTERN CAROLINA VINEGAR BBQ SAUCE:

- 1 cup apple cider vinegar
- 1 cup white vinegar
- 1 tablespoon red pepper flakes or more to taste
- 1 teaspoon black pepper
- ½ teaspoon salt

FOR WESTERN CAROLINA VINEGAR BBQ SAUCE:

- Same as above, plus add the following:
- ¼ cup ketchup
- 2 tablespoons tomato paste

DIRECTIONS

1. Heat all the ingredients to a large pan over medium-low heat. Simmer for 2–3 minutes. You can also use the microwave to warm it for 30 seconds, which is a common practice. Whisk it all together.

2. Transfer the vinegar barbecue sauce to a jar and let sit for 1 day to let the flavors meld.

3. Serve as desired.

HOT TIP

If you're serving with pulled pork, a general rule of thumb is to give each person about 2 tablespoons or 1 ounce of sauce. Too much sauce can overpower the meat!

What's the Difference Between North Carolina's Eastern and Western Barbecue Sauce?

The signature taste of North Carolina's eastern-style barbecue is that tangy, vinegary bite, while the western style is richer, sweeter, and has elements of tomato.

DUDE'S DYNAMITE BBQ SAUCE

SERVES 6

PREP TIME: 30 MINUTES | COOK TIME: 15 MINUTES
TIM OLIVER SCHNETTLER |
INGOLSTADT, BAVARIA, GERMANY

I lived in the US for a long time and have traveled the entire country as part of a culinary tour. Inspired by that, I simply wanted to create a spicy, fruity all-around barbecue sauce that goes well with fish and poultry, rounding out the flavor rather than overpowering it.

I experimented for six months and tested 250 variations before this recipe was finalized. Check out more of my barbecue recipes on Instagram (@the_barbecue_dude_official).

INGREDIENTS

- 1 cup water
- 1 cup sugar
- ½ cup vinegar
- 3 cloves garlic, minced
- ½ cup pineapple juice
- 2 tablespoons mustard
- 1 teaspoon turmeric
- 1 teaspoon red pepper flakes
- 1 onion, finely chopped
- 1 teaspoon cayenne pepper (or to taste)
- 1–2 chili peppers (depending on desired spiciness), chopped

DIRECTIONS

1. In a medium-sized saucepan, bring the water, sugar, and vinegar to a boil over medium heat, stirring until the sugar is completely dissolved.

2. Add the garlic, pineapple juice, mustard, turmeric, red pepper flakes, onion, and chili peppers.

3. Reduce the heat to low and let the sauce simmer for about 15–20 minutes until it slightly thickens and the flavors meld together.

4. If you desire a spicier sauce, you can add more cayenne pepper and season to taste.

5. Allow the barbecue sauce to cool, then pour it into a sealable jar or bottle.

GOOT OLE BBQ BEEF MARINADE

SERVES 2

PREP TIME: 15 MINUTES | COOK TIME: 1 HOUR, 15 MINUTES

ANGEL GUTIERREZ | CYPRESS, TEXAS

This was a recipe I created to improve the flavor of USDA select steaks. Prime steaks are amazing, but they are not always budget friendly. This will make about 1 cup of marinade and will be sufficient for one steak. This marinade also works well with beef kabobs and the marinating time is the same as the steak. If using for beef tenderloin, marinate overnight. This recipe can be double as needed for more steaks or whatever beef you cook.

INGREDIENTS

- ¼ cup brown sugar
- ¼ cup soy sauce
- 2 tablespoons Worcestershire sauce
- Juice of ½ a lemon
- ¼ teaspoon garlic powder
- ½ cup red wine vinegar

DIRECTIONS

1. Combine all the ingredients in a mixing bowl and whisk thoroughly.

2. Place the steak in a resealable plastic bag and pour in the marinade. Place in the refrigerator for minimum of 1 hour and no more than 6 hours.

3. Once you're ready to cook, the cook time is entirely your preference. I have done this with steaks, beef kabobs, and beef tenderloin and it's fantastic!

GOOT OLE BBQ TURKEY BRINE

SERVES 6

PREP TIME: 15 MINUTES | COOK TIME: 45 MINUTES

ANGEL GUTIERREZ | CYPRESS, TEXAS

This a recipe I created over time testing out different flavors to make the best tasting turkey legs. It was a challenge my brother put up, so I was more than willing to take it on. Today, this brine is used for my chickens in barbecue competitions.

INGREDIENTS

- 1 gallon water
- 1 cup kosher salt
- ½ cup brown sugar
- 2 tablespoons onion powder
- 2 tablespoons chili powder
- 1 tablespoon garlic powder
- 1 tablespoon paprika
- 1 tablespoon ground pepper
- 1 teaspoon ground cumin
- 3 sprigs of rosemary
- 6 medium-sized turkey legs

Note: If you have more than 6 medium-sized turkey legs to cook, simply double the recipe as much as needed.

DIRECTIONS

1. Combine all ingredients in a large pot and whisk thoroughly. Put on high heat and bring the brine to a boil. Stir occasionally and once it comes to a boil, allow it to boil for 5 minutes, then turn off heat.

2. Cool the brine down to room temperature. Add ice to the brine to speed up the cooling process. This will not affect the flavor of the brine.

3. Once cooled, place your turkey legs in a pot or brine bucket, then pour the brine over the turkey legs. Make sure they are fully submerged in the brine.

4. Put a lid on it and place in the refrigerator. You want the legs sitting in the brine at minimum overnight or up to 24 hours.

5. Once you're ready to cook the legs, pull them out of the brine and place them on a preheated smoker. Smoke them between 250°F and 275°F. My preferred wood choice is hickory.

6. Turn legs over every hour to hour and a half until it reaches an internal temperature of 165°F. (Cook time will vary based on your smoker and the weather.)

SAN FRANCISCO BBQ SAUCE

SERVES 6

PREP TIME: 15 MINUTES | COOK TIME: 15 MINUTES

JOHN MARDIKIAN | SAN FRANCISCO, CALIFORNIA

Whenever I serve this sauce, guests always lick their fingers, and I've even seen some eat it with a spoon! It's a spin on the fusion food movement, which brought together Eastern and Western techniques and ingredients, resulting in a cuisine that captures the best of both styles. It can be made quickly and has a long shelf life in the fridge. It goes great on everything, but I love it on pork ribs. I recently served it with slow roasted pork ribs that were seared on charcoal and the meat was put into a bao bun with pickled carrots and daikon (recipe on page 99). This sauce can also be brushed onto meats as they crisp on the grill and when it caramelizes, it will create fans everywhere it goes.

INGREDIENTS

- One 9-ounce jar plum sauce
- 1 cup hoisin sauce
- 1 cup orange juice
- ½ bunch cilantro
- 3 cloves garlic
- 2 tablespoons minced fresh ginger

DIRECTIONS

1. Finley chop the ½ bunch of cilantro. (It's okay to use most of the stems as well). Chop the cloves of garlic and ginger.

2. Mix together with the hoisin sauce, plum sauce, and orange juice. Sauce can be stored in the fridge for however long the shelf life of the orange juice was!

Is Bone-In Better?

There is a common belief that bone-in steaks offer more flavor than boneless. However, the marrow of the bone—which gives extra flavor—can only travel a few fractions of an inch, so there is really no difference in flavor. The main differences in grilling steaks are aesthetics and insulation. The meat around the bone will cook slower than the rest of the steak.

SAVORY SWEET DRY RUB FOR RIBS

SERVES 7+

PREP TIME: 15 MINUTES

ELIZABETH MARTINS | PHILADELPHIA, PENNSYLVANIA

This has become our family's ultimate go-to rub recipe, thanks to its irresistible fusion of ancho chili powder and paprika, infusing our ribs with a smoky depth of flavor that never fails to impress. Plus, the harmonious blend of dark brown sugar and kosher salt strikes the perfect balance, enhancing every bite with a satisfyingly sweet and savory touch, making our barbecues truly unforgettable! Whether you're a family on the go or a host planning a summer barbecue, this Savory Sweet Dry Rub for Ribs will become your culinary companion.

INGREDIENTS

- 1 cup dark brown sugar
- ¼ cup kosher salt
- 2 tablespoons paprika
- 2 tablespoons ancho chili powder
- 2 tablespoons coarse black pepper (Substitute: You can use 2 tablespoons ground pepper as well; the coarse pepper will just provide more texture)
- 2 tablespoons dry mustard
- ½ tablespoon granulated garlic (Substitute: 1 teaspoon garlic powder)
- 1 teaspoon onion powder (Substitute: 3 teaspoons dried minced onion)

DIRECTIONS

MIX IT UP:

1. Grab a big bowl and blend all the ingredients together. Give it a good stir until they're all intertwined.
2. Pop your flavorful creation into a mason jar and stash it in a cool, dark place.

RUB IT IN:

3. Go ahead and give those pork cuts a hearty rubdown with your special blend. For a cozy fit, start with a little olive oil to help the rub stick nicely to the meat.

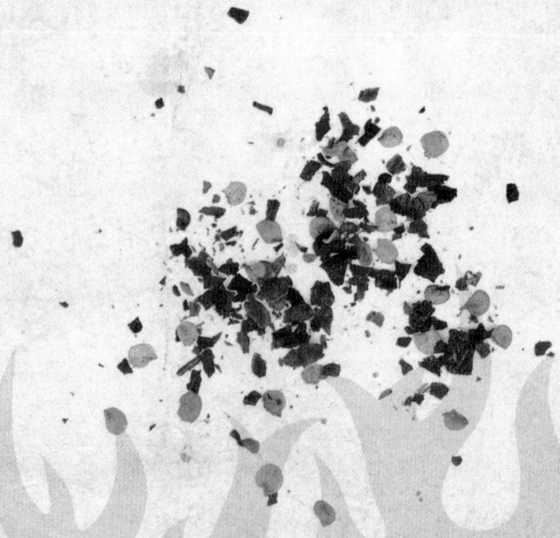

TRACI'S HOMEMADE BBQ SAUCE

SERVES 7+

PREP TIME: 15 MINUTES | COOK TIME: 15 MINUTES
TRACI ANTONOVICH | SONOMA COUNTY, CALIFORNIA

This mouthwatering, homemade barbecue sauce recipe was created out of my necessity to find a last-minute condiment to slather over chicken, beef, or pork, whether grilled or smoked. We tested this sauce several times, made adjustments, and here we are with the best homemade barbecue sauce for all the things! The heat and sweet flavors are perfectly balanced for a 30-minute recipe, but this saucy number gets even better by the day!

INGREDIENTS

- ¼ cup apple cider vinegar
- ¼ cup honey or brown sugar
- 1 tablespoon molasses or brown sugar
- 2 tablespoons Worcestershire sauce
- 2 teaspoons paprika
- 2 teaspoons onion powder
- 1 teaspoon garlic powder
- ½ teaspoon chili powder
- ¼ teaspoon black pepper
- ½ teaspoon sea salt

DIRECTIONS

1. Combine all ingredients in a sauce pot and cook over medium-high heat until the mixture starts to bubble, stirring as needed.

2. Reduce heat to medium-low and simmer 10–20 minutes until it thickens to your liking, stirring as needed.

3. Serve warm or cold.

Note: To store, cool sauce to room temperature. Refrigerate in an airtight container up to 1 week or 30–60 days in the freezer.

SWEET TREATS

You've had a hefty meal of barbecue, but now you need something sweet! These desserts are perfect for a summer cookout and offer just the right sweet and tangy flavor profile to enjoy after a hearty pulled pork sandwich or a savory rack of ribs.

LEMON MERINGUE CUPCAKES

MINT-LEMONADE POPSICLES

STRAWBERRY-RHUBARB CRUMBLE

WATERMELON GRANITA

LEMON MERINGUE CUPCAKES

MAKES 12

PREP TIME: 30 MINUTES | COOK TIME: 10–15 MINUTES

SUE MCMAHON | BECKENHAM, KENT, ENGLAND

The lemon in these cupcakes gives a fresh citrus tang that goes perfectly with a zingy fruit topping. The meringue on top is an Italian-style meringue, which is smoother than the traditional meringue made from whisked egg whites and sugar.

INGREDIENTS

LEMON CUPCAKES:
- 9 tablespoons butter, softened
- ½ cup superfine sugar
- 2 medium eggs
- Finely grated zest and juice of 1 lemon
- 1 cup self-rising flour

LEMON CURD TOPPING:
- 5–7 tablespoons lemon curd
- Piping bag fitted with star piping tip

MERINGUE:
- 3½ tablespoons water
- ¾ cup superfine sugar
- 1 tablespoon light corn syrup
- 3 large egg whites

DIRECTIONS

LEMON CUPCAKES:
1. Preheat oven to 375°F.
2. Beat the butter and sugar together in a bowl until the mixture is light and fluffy. Add the eggs, lemon zest, lemon juice, and flour to the bowl and beat the mixture until smooth.
3. Divide the mixture among the cupcake liners and bake in the center of the oven until the cakes have risen and are just firm to the touch in the center. Standard-size cupcakes will take about 12 to 15 minutes and mini cakes about 10 to 12 minutes.
4. Remove the cakes from the oven and transfer them to a wire rack to cool.

LEMON CURD TOPPING:
1. Spread the lemon curd over the tops of the cupcakes and place them on a baking tray.

MERINGUE:
1. Pour the water into a small saucepan and add the sugar.
2. Place the pan over medium heat and stir until the sugar has dissolved.
3. Add the light corn syrup to the pan and stir briefly until dissolved.
4. Wash down any sugar crystals on the side of the pan with a damp pastry brush.
5. Increase the heat and boil the mixture rapidly until it reaches 248°F, occasionally washing down the sides of the pan.
6. Meanwhile whisk the egg whites until stiff.
7. When the sugar has reached the correct temperature, remove the pan from the heat and plunge the base of the pan into a bowl of cold water to stop the cooking process.
8. With an electric mixer running at slow speed, gradually pour the syrup over the egg whites. Continue whisking at high speed until the mixture cools.
9. Fill a piping bag fitted with a star piping tip with the meringue mixture and swirl over the lemon curd.
10. Bake the cakes in the center of the oven for 2 to 3 minutes, or until the meringue is a light golden color.
11. Remove from the oven and serve immediately or within 2 hours.

SWEET TREATS

MINT-LEMONADE POPSICLES

SERVES 10

PREP TIME: 10 MINUTES | **COOK TIME:** 6 HOURS

BRIANNE GRAJKOWSKI | SAN DIEGO, CALIFORNIA

After enjoying savory barbecue, your guests will love these cold, refreshing treats during your summer cookout!

INGREDIENTS

- 5 cups water
- 1 cup granulated sugar
- 4 lemons
- ½ cup mint

DIRECTIONS

1. Make a simple syrup by boiling the sugar in 1 cup of water in a small saucepan on medium heat.

2. Squeeze the juice of all four lemons into a blender and add mint. Blend mint and lemon juice for 1 minute.

3. Strain lemon-mint juice into a pitcher.

4. Pour simple syrup into the pitcher with remaining water and stir.

5. Pour into popsicle molds and freeze for 6 hours.

6. Serve!

HOT TIP

Strain the mint out of the lemon juice after blending to keep mint leaves out of the popsicles!

STRAWBERRY-RHUBARB CRUMBLE

SERVES 12–16

PREP TIME: 20 MINUTES | COOK TIME: 50 MINUTES | SERVES 12–16

KAYLA BUTTS | ROCKPORT, TEXAS

Much of my focus in the kitchen is devoted to saving my most precious resource: time. Many of my recipes have minimal active time, and instead let the ingredients or the oven do most of the work. This crumble is no exception. Strawberry and rhubarb create their own syrup while languishing in sugar (while you languish on the couch).

INGREDIENTS

FRUIT FILLING:
- 2 cups rhubarb, diced
- 2 cups strawberries, chopped
- ⅔ cup sugar
- ¼ teaspoon salt
- ¼ cup all-purpose flour
- 1 tablespoon butter, melted
- 1 teaspoon vanilla extract

CRUMBLE TOPPING:
- 1½ cups all-purpose flour
- 1 cup brown sugar
- ½ teaspoons cinnamon
- ¼ teaspoons nutmeg
- ¼ teaspoon salt
- ½ cup butter, cubed
- Optional: vanilla ice cream, for serving

DIRECTIONS

FRUIT FILLING:
1. Preheat the oven to 350°F.
2. Combine the rhubarb, strawberries, and sugar in a large bowl and let it sit for 15 minutes, stirring occasionally.
3. Sprinkle the salt and flour onto the rhubarb mixture before adding the butter and vanilla. Mix well until the rhubarb and berries are coated and the flour has dissolved.
4. Transfer it to an 8 x 8-inch baking dish.

CRUMBLE TOPPING:
5. Whisk the flour, brown sugar, cinnamon, nutmeg, and salt together in a medium bowl.
6. Using a fork or a pastry blender, cut in the butter until the mixture resembles oatmeal. Distribute the crumble topping evenly over the prepared filling.
7. Bake the crumble in the oven for 50 minutes, until the filling is bubbly and the topping is golden brown. Check crumble at 35 minutes and, if the outer edge of the topping is already browned, cover it with aluminum foil.
8. Serve warm with vanilla ice cream.

SWEET TREATS

WATERMELON GRANITA

SERVES 12

PREP TIME: 2 HOURS | COOK TIME: 2 MINUTES

KAYLA BUTTS | ROCKPORT, TEXAS

This granita is a lovely dish originally from Sicily. This frozen fruit dessert could be the love child of sorbet and shaved ice. Granita requires no special equipment or ingredients, only a little patience while the fruit slurry freezes.

INGREDIENTS

- ¾ cup water
- ½ cup sugar
- 7 cups peeled and cubed watermelon
- 4 tablespoons lime juice (or juice of 2 limes)
- Small bunch fresh sweet basil (about 6 large leaves)

DIRECTIONS

1. Place a 9 x 13-inch glass or metal dish in the freezer.

2. Place the water and sugar in a small saucepan over medium-high heat. Simmer while stirring with a whisk until all of the sugar is dissolved and the liquid reaches a syrup consistency, about 2 minutes. Let it cool to room temperature.

3. Combine the watermelon, simple syrup (the water and sugar mixture), lime, and basil in a food processor and pulse until smooth.

4. Pour the mixture into the cooled pan and place it back in the freezer.

5. Using a whisk, stir mixture every 20 minutes, until the desired consistency is reached, before serving.

6. Scoop into small cups and serve cold.

SWEET TREATS

THIRST
QUENCHERS

Every good meal deserves a delicious drink. Whether you booze it up or not, options abound and all pair perfectly with barbecue!

ALCOHOLIC:

PEACH BOWL

WINE CUP

NONALCOHOLIC:

BOOZE-FREE PENICILLIN

CRANBERRY COOLER

LAVENDER LEMONADE

POM BASIL SHRUB

STRAWBERRY DAIQUIRI

FENNEL RASPBERRY MARTINI

PEACH BOWL

DAVID BIGGS | CAPE TOWN, SOUTH AFRICA

SERVES
20

Before the guests arrive, prepare for this delicious drink by peeling the peaches, cutting them into slices, and leaving them to steep in brandy.

INGREDIENTS

- 6 very ripe peaches, rinsed and sliced
- 3 bottles of chilled champagne or dry sparkling wine
- ½ cup brandy
- Sugar, to taste

DIRECTIONS

1. Place the peach slices in a large punch bowl and sprinkle with sugar. Add the brandy and leave to stand until just before the guests arrive.

2. When the first guests arrive, pour the champagne or dry sparkling wine into a bowl and ladle a helping into each glass over ice.

WINE CUP

DAVID BIGGS | CAPE TOWN, SOUTH AFRICA

MAKES
1 PITCHER

Before the guests arrive, prepare for this delicious drink by peeling the peaches, cutting them into slices, and leaving them to steep in brandy.

INGREDIENTS

- 1 bottle chilled dry white wine
- ½ cup diced fresh pineapple
- Peel of half an orange cut into strips
- ½ cup medium cream sherry
- 1 quart soda water
- Optional: orange slices

DIRECTIONS

1. Pour chilled dry white wine into a tall pitcher with the diced fresh pineapple, orange peels, and medium cream sherry. If desired, also add orange slices.

2. Allow the mixture to stand until needed, then top up the pitcher with soda water and stir gently.

3. Serve with ice.

THIRST QUENCHERS (ALCOHOLIC)

BOOZE-FREE PENICILLIN

SERVES 1

DOUGLAS WATTERS | NEW YORK, NEW YORK

The penicillin is one of my very favorite cocktails, and its smoky flavor complements barbecue nicely. The fresh lemon juice, smoky and peaty Islay malt Scotch whiskey, and the bit of sweetness and bite from the ginger liqueur is just about perfect. The decadent, woody smoothness and hint of black pepper spice of Three Spirit Nightcap holds up well as an alternative for the Scotch.

INGREDIENTS

- 2 ounces Three Spirit Nightcap
- 1 ounce fresh-squeezed lemon juice
- ¾ ounce ginger syrup
- Ice
- Candied ginger and lemon peel, for garnish

DIRECTIONS

1. Combine all ingredients in an ice-filled cocktail shaker or mason jar.
2. Shake hard and strain into an ice-filled whiskey tumbler.
3. Garnish with candied ginger and lemon peel.

CRANBERRY COOLER

SERVES 1

A tasty treat for all ages, this mocktail is tart, refreshing, and easy to whip up quickly!

INGREDIENTS

- 1 part cranberry juice
- 1 splash lime cordial
- 1 part ginger ale
- Slice of lemon, for garnish
- Crushed ice

DIRECTIONS

1. Pour the cranberry juice, lime cordial, and ginger ale over crushed ice in a tall glass.
2. Stir gently and garnish with a slice of lemon.

LAVENDER LEMONADE

SERVES 8

DAVID BIGGS | CAPE TOWN, SOUTH AFRICA

This upmarket twist on traditional lemonade looks as good as it tastes!

INGREDIENTS

- 8 cups water
- 1 cup sugar
- 1½ cups juice from a lemon
- 10 sprigs fresh lavender

DIRECTIONS

1. Boil water.
2. Add sugar and simmer on low heat for 5 to 7 minutes, stirring often.
3. When the sugar is dissolved, remove from heat and add lemon juice and lavender.
4. Let the lemonade cool to room temperature, remove the lavender sprigs, and refrigerate in a pitcher overnight.
5. When ready for guests, serve over ice!

Optional: Cut more lemon slices and place in pitcher before serving or as a garnish, along with a fresh lavender sprig.

POM BASIL SHRUB

SERVES 1

BILL GAMELLI | NEW YORK, NEW YORK

This is a refreshing sangria alternative that blends sweet and tart pomegranate flavor with basil and balsamic vinegar.

INGREDIENTS

- 1 bottle Mocktails Sansgria
- 3 tablespoons fresh pomegranate seeds
- 6 fresh basil leaves
- 1 teaspoon. balsamic vinegar
- Ice
- 1 bunch basil, for garnish

DIRECTIONS

1. Add the pomegranate seeds, basil leaves, balsamic vinegar, and a splash of Sansgria to a cocktail shaker and muddle well.
2. Fill ⅓ of the cocktail shaker with ice and shake vigorously for 5 to 8 seconds.
3. Pour into a large wine glass or goblet and garnish with basil.

STRAWBERRY DAQUIRI

SERVES 1

The fresh strawberry flavor blends perfectly with the sour mix in this alcohol-free version of a classic bar favorite. Note: If you make this with a traditional sour mix (featuring egg white), pregnant women and the elderly should avoid drinking.

INGREDIENTS

- 3 ounces fresh or frozen strawberries
- 1 splash sour mix
- 1 dash grenadine
- Ice cubes
- Fresh fruit, for garnish

DIRECTIONS

1. In a blender, mix all ingredients until smooth.
2. Pour into your preferred glass and garnish with fresh fruit.

FENNEL RASPBERRY MARTINI

BILL GAMELLI | NEW YORK, NEW YORK

This refreshing drink muddles together warm, sweet aniseed flavors and aromas with the fresh tartness of raspberry and a bite of sour lime.

INGREDIENTS

- 1 bottle Mocktails Mockapolitan
- ½ teaspoon fennel seeds
- 1 star anise pod
- 8 fresh raspberries, plus more for garnish
- 1 teaspoon freshly squeezed lime juice
- Ice

DIRECTIONS

1. Add the fennel seeds, star anise, fresh raspberries, and lime juice to a cocktail shaker and muddle together to form a pulp.
2. Add ice to fill ⅓ of the shaker.
3. Add the entire bottle of Mockapolitan and shake vigorously for 5 to 8 seconds.
4. Strain into a martini glass and garnish with fresh raspberries.

THIRST QUENCHERS (NONALCOHOLIC)

ABOUT THE CONTRIBUTORS

2Chefs

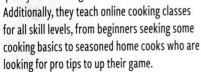

2Chefs are a husband-and-wife private chef team who prepare healthy weekly meals for their clients using quality seasonal ingredients. Additionally, they teach online cooking classes for all skill levels, from beginners seeking some cooking basics to seasoned home cooks who are looking for pro tips to up their game.

Antonovich, Traci

Traci owns and operates The Kitchen Girl website featuring delicious recipes written during her 14 years of professional food industry experience, two years of culinary arts, and decades of home cooking. Her followers love her use of simple ingredients and straightforward instructions. When it comes to barbecue, she loves sharing her standout sides and sauces. These recipes are available, along with expert tips, on her website, www.thekitchengirl.com.

Batten, Dante

Dante Batten is the founder of Rosa's Southern BBQ and Utopia Culinary Management, founded in 2015. His organization supports underserved communities through culinary programs and sponsorships. Dante has over 20 years in the food service and barbecue arena!

Biggs, David

(Not pictured.) David Biggs, born and raised in South Africa, joined the reporting staff of a country newspaper in 1965 and discovered his affinity for wine after moving to Cape Town. He has written a weekly wine column for a daily newspaper for more than 20 years, and has published several books on the subject, among them the annual *Plonk Buyer's Guide*. David Biggs is the author of *Cocktails & After Dinner Drinks*, *Make Your Own Cocktails*, *The Cocktail Handbook*, *Legendary Cocktails*, and *Sharp Shooters*.

Bonifacic, Marc

(Not pictured.) New Orleans' favorite barbecue restaurant may be newer to the city than some, but its time-honored recipes were honed through decades of dedication to the culinary craft of barbecuing. Central City BBQ became a reality after decades of friendship between Aaron Burgau, an award-winning chef and owner of Restaurant Patois, and his Jesuit classmate, Marc Bonifacic, a third-generation restaurant owner whose grandfather operated a family-owned barbecue shop and passed on his passion and expertise in the art of barbecuing on to him.

Bringle, Carey

Carey Bringle is a restaurant owner (Peg Leg Porker, Bringle's Smoking Oasis, and Pig Star), award-winning spirits company owner (Peg Leg Porker Bourbon), author (*BBQ for Dummies*), and pitmaster in Nashville, TN. He's been smoking barbecue for 30+ years, including competing annually in Memphis In May International BBQ Festival. He has three children, an amazing wife who has her own all-female whole hog cook team (I Only Smoke When I Drink), and two English Bulldogs. Carey has one leg (he lost the other one to cancer when he was 17), which is where the name Peg Leg Porker came from—he is the Peg Leg Porker.

Butts, Kayla

Kayla Butts is a professional dietitian, cooking and nutrition instructor, small-scale Texas farmer, a clinical nutrition manager with a Master's in Science in Nutrition, and cookbook author of *Garden to Table*.

Camp, Troy

Troy Camp, aka Bandit, is the owner, head pitmaster, and rub and sauce maker for the award-winning competition barbecue team, Bandits' Backyard BBQ. He started cooking as a very young man after watching his grandma in the kitchen. In 2017, Troy jumped into the professional barbecue circuit and has been competing against the best in the world ever since. In 2018, his team released their own line of barbecue rubs and sauces that are available in several retail stores and online.

Cruz-Peters, Ramona

Ramona Cruz-Peters is a two-time published cookbook author and the founder and Editor-in-Chief of lifestyle website and social media presence, Fab Everyday. She currently lives in Texas, but her barbecue experience comes from her Puerto Rican father, who taught her about seasoning, marinading, smoking, and grilling to perfection using some of their favorite Caribbean-style seasonings.

Fanelli, Mike

Mike Fanelli (@godfather_of_meat) is a content creator on both Instagram and TikTok with nearly 350,000 followers across all social media platforms. He loves to cook and visit great food establishments for his audience.

Faraz

(Not pictured.) According to Faraz, "Persians take food very seriously, and if you've ever tried Persian food, this will confirm my statement." With that being said, he'd like to introduce you to Joojeh Kababs!

Figaro, Nate

Nate Figaro is a self-taught pitmaster that specializes in Southeast, Louisiana-style Creole barbecue. He focuses on using spices and herbs found in both Caribbean and Spanish cultures and dishes he ate growing up in Louisiana. He started his barbecue journey reading cookbooks and burning a lot of meat. Eventually, Nate got better, but knew he needed to improve his skills, so he decided to work on a barbecue food truck. From there, Nate worked at another brick-and-mortar barbecue restaurant. Inspired by the barbecue he grew up eating made by his grandfather, he started creating his own rubs. Eventually, he made his Creole barbecue rub and started giving out samples to coworkers. After multiple requests to do plate lunches, on the weekends, he would smoke pork butts, ribs, and briskets and sell them to neighbors and friends. This year, Nate was selected to participate in Kingsford Preserve the Pit, a program that recognizes the impact African Americans have on the history of barbecue. Kingsford selects African American pitmasters from around the US and pairs them with a famous pitmaster as a mentorship. Currently, he's in the process of setting up barbecue pop-ups and eventually getting a food trailer for his business.

Finn, Pedr

Pedr Finn is a chef with over 20 years of experience in the food industry and a degree in Journalism. He has been based in Vietnam for the past 11 years, living and breathing Vietnamese food, culture, and lifestyle, and working as a chef, restaurateur, freelance food journalist, tour guide, and food content writer.

Fuchs, Matthew

Matthew Fuchs got into barbecue with an Oklahoma Joe's Highland Offset Smoker just as the pandemic was starting. He always had a passion for barbecue, but never had the time seriously to work on his craft. Once the pandemic hit, it left him with time to work on his skills. Matthew took the leap and invested in a Franklin BBQ Pit and the rest was history. His family restaurant gave him the opportunity to utilize his passion for Central Texas barbecue at his American grill and brewpub.

Gamelli, Bill

Former Wall Street executive Bill Gamelli and his two co-founding partners, Mark Guthrie and Jim Dowla, created Mocktail Beverages in 2018 to create healthy, sophisticated beverages catering to every guest at a party—the nondrinker, the mindful drinker, and everyone else. They worked with global award-winning mixologist Ezra Star to create their initial range of four variants. The Mocktails mixologists have spent years sourcing and combining 100% natural, sustainable, and ethically sourced botanicals to arrive at the delicious, complex, and tantalizing balance of flavors in every Mocktails drink.

Grajkowski, Brianne

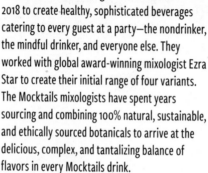

Brianne Grajkowski is the founder, creative director and editor-in-chief of BriGeeski, Inc., a food-focused lifestyle blog and online media agency. Bri features everyday recipes, adventures, travel, design, and party tips on the So Cal-based blog. Bri won Puesto's Next Top Taco contest and had her taco recipe on their menu as a special of the month. Bri is a home cook, who learned from watching her family and tasting food from local restaurants for her blog. She's determined to teach her kids how to cook at an early age and help other families come together in the kitchen too. Bri's first cookbook, *Cooking With Kids,* is a great way to get your kids involved in cooking too! Bri's Best BBQ Chicken Drumsticks are one of the top recipes on her blog and their family is known for serving the best tri-tip around!

Grove, Chris

Chris Grove has a published barbecue blog for 15 years, two published barbecue books (Ulysses Press), has a competitive barbecue /grilling team, and is a 3x certified food judge.

Gutierrez, Angel

Angel Gutierrez has been in barbecue since 2014. He has competed in many cook-offs, with the Houston Rodeo Cook-Off being his biggest competition. In 2021, Angel started his barbecue catering business and has catered birthday parties, wedding receptions, and even a business grand opening.

Hanger, Jordan

Jordan Hanger is an outdoor cooking and grilling enthusiast with recipes that focus on bold flavors any person can make at home. His favorite thing about food is that it brings people together. Jordan loves to develop new recipes and fuse different dishes together to make food better. Growing up with an American dad and a Korean mom, he came to love and appreciate a wide variety of food, especially Asian and American barbecue. Thus, TheNinjacue.com was born!

Helmer, Jodi

Jodi Helmer is an experienced journalist who writes about food, gardening, farming, the environment, and sustainable living. Jodi's work has appeared in *Entrepreneur, Hemispheres, Civil Eats, National Geographic Traveler, AARP, Farm Life, WebMD, Health, CNNMoney,* and *Guardian Sustainable Business.* She is the author of five books, including *Growing Your Own Cocktails, Mocktails, Teas & Infusions, The Green Year,* and *Farm Fresh Georgia.* When she's not writing, she's growing vegetables and raising bees.

Horn, Matt

Chef and restaurateur Matt Horn is a leading authority on barbecue and a rising star in the US restaurant scene overall, drawing acclaim from barbecue aficionados and media across the nation with his own California style. In October 2020, he opened his first restaurant, Horn Barbecue, in Oakland, CA, which drew instant acclaim from loyal fans and both local and national media, followed by the 2022 opening of his sophomore concept, Kowbird, and his first elevated dining concept, Matty's Old Fashioned in 2023. In 2021, Matt Horn was named one of *Food & Wine's* Best New Chefs in America, and Horn Barbecue was named one of *Esquire Magazine's* Best New Restaurants in America and landed a coveted Michelin Bib Gourmand designation. In 2022, Horn Barbecue was nominated for a James Beard Award, in the Best New Restaurant category. Chef Horn was recently named to the Williams Sonoma Chefs Collective (2023), is a YETI Chef Ambassador and Chef Partner for Made In Cookware.

Hudson, Leo

Leo Hudson is an Arizona transplant from Missouri and he loves Kansas City style barbecue. Perfecting his barbecue recipes was an every weekend event. Trying out new meats, dry rubs, sauces, and cooking strategies was just a way of life. After moving to Arizona, he began to expand his culinary skills and started using barbecue in other recipes to give them a little extra smoke and flavor. If there's ever any leftover barbecue, it's going in a chili, or being used for a pizza, or going into a chopped salad—there's never any barbecue that goes to waste in his household. Being around people who didn't have the privilege of having such amazing barbecue for most of their lives made Leo feel like he was spreading the gospel of good barbecue in Arizona. It's a rough and tasty job, but someone has to do it!

Hultquist, Mike

Mike Hultquist is a food blogger at ChiliPepper Madness.com where he specializes in spicy cuisine, and he has been barbecuing since he learned to cook! He built a nice backyard kitchen where he loves to spend his days. Mike is the author of *The Spicy Food Lovers' Cookbook* and *The Spicy Dehydrator Cookbook*.

Jennine

(Not pictured.) Barbecue has brought Jennine's extended family together for years. To her, reuniting with cousins, grandparents, aunts, and uncles is always a great time with great food!

Khalifé, Maria

Maria Khalifé is an acclaimed celebrity chef, cookbook author, and television personality in Lebanon and other Arab countries. She is the founder and owner of Soufra Daimeh Food Network, the first food channel in the Arab world. Maria also started the first private cookery school in Lebanon, offering a variety of local and international cookery courses taught by talented chefs and cookbook authors.

Langston, Waylon

(Not pictured.) Waylon Langston is 12 years old and makes cooking videos online on his YouTube channel, WayWayAwesome.

Lattore, Achunchigan

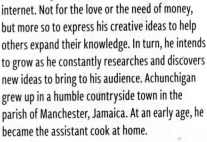

Achunchigan Lattore once had aspirations of being a chef. Today, he is quite content sharing his passion with the world through the power of the internet. Not for the love or the need of money, but more so to express his creative ideas to help others expand their knowledge. In turn, he intends to grow as he constantly researches and discovers new ideas to bring to his audience. Achunchigan grew up in a humble countryside town in the parish of Manchester, Jamaica. At an early age, he became the assistant cook at home.

Lee, Jiyeon

Jiyeon Lee is the chef and owner of Heirloom Market BBQ in Atlanta with chef Cody Taylor since 2010.

Letchworth, Michael

Michael Letchworth is the owner and operator of Sam Jones BBQ. They have two locations and a retail company. He has been part of the barbecue business in some form for the past 20 years. Michael started working at the iconic Skylight Inn BBQ in high school and through college. After a five-year break of helping with catering or events, he returned to the Jones' family traditions to partner with Samuel Jones to open Sam Jones BBQ in 2015.

Lovette, Jane

Jane Lovett is an experienced cook who trained at the Cordon Bleu in London and then at Leith's in the UK. She is a food stylist, recipe developer, and author with over 40 years of experience and has her own successful catering business with a number of high-profile clients.

Lundberg, Sara

Sara Lundberg is a proud mom of five wonderful children and has been a passionate lover of barbecue since her early years. Fond memories flood her mind of grilling mouthwatering burgers and chicken alongside her dad, while savoring a refreshing soda. On top of that, Sara has been fortunate enough to achieve significant milestones as a published cookbook writer, victorious cooking competition participant, and dedicated blogger for budgetsavvydiva.com.

Maddie & Kiki

Maddie & Kiki, Canada's favorite female Grill Masters, were named in the Top 10 Grill Experts of North America and are regularly featured in the prestigious *Forbes Magazine*. Barbecue industry professionals turn to Maddie & Kiki for consultation, where they share their knowledge, expertise, and input in the development of new products for the barbecue market. Maddie & Kiki teach barbecue classes in-person at their Grill Studio, as well as virtually across the globe. The sisters have traveled across the US and Canada, appearing on morning shows, podcasts, radio, and live events, inspiring people of all ages to fall in love with the art of outdoor cookery.

Mardikian, John

John Mardikian has always loved food and he's been lucky to spend decades of his life cooking and working in the restaurant business. There's nothing that speaks more to him than the deep love hidden within the flavor or great barbecue.

Martins, Elizabeth

Hailing from Philadelphia, Elizabeth is a writer and musician. She loves cooking with her family— it's not just about meals but creating cherished moments with laughter and conversation.

McMahon, Sue

Sue McMahon is Cookery Editor for *Woman's Weekly* magazine. Although she's happy to take on the challenge of any culinary recipe, her passion is cakes and she travels the world teaching cake decorating. Over the last few years she has demonstrated in America, Malaysia, and Japan, as well as in several European countries. Sue is a member of the Guild of Food Writers, Craft Guild of Chefs, and the British Sugarcraft Guild.

Miller, Sean

Sean Miller has been smoking meat for friends, family, and groups since he got his first smoker in 2011. He loves *The Office* and watched it live and, of course, has rewatched the show multiple times since! He's also passionate about making the best barbecue people can possibly eat. Sean has built and maintained active barbecue social media accounts since 2017 with over 120,000 followers and over 20 million views.

Nevarez, Kelli

Kelli Nevarez started in barbecue as a team member of her parents', Lupe and Christine's, cook-off team. She later turned in her second-grade classroom keys for a pit room key. Today, Kelli continues this partnership as a co-owner and pitmaster of Lavaca BBQ. With her dad's training and her own female intuition, Kelli helped secure their restaurant, LaVaca BBQ in Port Lavaca, Texas, as one of *Texas Monthly Magazine's* 2021 Top 50 Best BBQ Joints in Texas. She has been highlighted by *EATER New York* and was also in the August 2023 issue of *Southern Living* magazine.

O'Leary, Dermot

(Not pictured.) Dermot O'Leary, radio and TV presenter, is best known as *The X Factor* front man. He lives in London and along with close friends, James Ginzler and Paul Shovlin, is passionate about good food and locally-sourced, in-season fish and seafood.

Perel, Ryan

Ryan Perel is a gluten-free home cook living in Dallas, TX and he loves to eat barbecue.

Raichlen, Steven

Author, journalist, lecturer, and TV host, Steven Raichlen is the man who launched the barbecue revolution. Raichlen's books (more than 6 million copies in print) have won five James Beard Awards and three IACP Julia Child Awards and have been translated into 17 languages. He hosts the popular TV shows, *Steven Raichlen's Project Fire, Project Smoke, Primal Grill,* and *Barbecue University,* as well as his latest show, *Steven Raichlen's Planet Barbecue.* An award-winning journalist, Raichlen writes regularly for *The New York Times.* His work has appeared in *The Wall Street Journal, Esquire, GQ,* and all the major food magazines. In 2015, he was inducted into the KCBS Barbecue Hall of Fame. His websites are stevenraichlen.com and barbecuebible.com.

Reinhardt, Rob

Rob Reinhardt is a Canadian National BBQ Champion, with over 300 awards in barbecue collected from all over the world. He spends his summers serving barbecue to the biggest crowds in Canada and loves every minute of it. In the off-season, Rob teaches barbecue classes and develops recipes and barbecue seasonings.

Romero, Ava Marie

Chef Ava Marie Romero is a food blogger and award-winning competition home cook born with autism. She's an at-home barbecue sauce and rub expert, and as a Californian, she finds ways to barbecue indoors. As a 2018 Dessert Finalist at the World Food Championship, she has met celebrities, including Guy Fieri, Jet Tila, and even comedian Pete Lee from *The Tonight Show* starring Jimmy Fallon.

Ruiz, Marcus

Growing up, the men Marcus Ruiz aspired to be used to gather around a barbecue pit on Saturday evenings with the biggest smiles on their faces. His dad would man the grill and one day, he let Marcus help him. He was anxious about it, but when they served the food, there was a silence that swaddled the room when everyone began to eat, and Marcus became addicted to it. He has loved learning the traditions from his family members and has

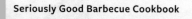

now become the person to pass it on to the next generation. There's an art to barbecue and he absolutely loves it.

Schnettler, Tim Oliver

Tim Oliver Schnettler is The Barbecue Dude! He runs one of the most successful European barbecue social media profiles (@the_barbecue_dude_official), reaching an average of 80 million contacts worldwide every month. In terms of engagement rates, he's regularly ranked number one globally. Followers love his exciting recipe developments and the often new and surprising approaches.

Shackleford, Cory

Growing up in California, most of Cory Shackleford's nights and weekends were full of barbecue and family!

Sheehan, Ray

Ray Sheehan is an award-winning barbecue sauce maker, recipe developer, and two-time cookbook author. He's also a certified Kansas City Barbecue Society judge, member of the National Barbecue and Grilling Association, and 9x winner of the Award of Excellence from the National Barbecue Association. A chef by trade, Ray has been in the food business for over 25 years. Since 2017, he has been a contributor to *Barbecue News Magazine*, providing recipes, articles, and product reviews.

Sherin, Dustin

Two years ago, Dustin Sherin got the best smoker made in Tulsa, Oklahoma, USA—Hasty Bake Legacy 131—and he can't stop smoking for EVERY occasion. Friends, family, it doesn't matter—he loves to make barbecue.

Sikora, Jennifer

Jennifer Sikora is a lover of all things barbecue! As a newbie, she could only make barbecue in the oven or slow cooker. But now, she has ventured outside and has been making barbecue on her grill, The Blackstone, and soon . . . her new smoker. Jennifer loves making delicious finger-licking barbecue recipes to share with her family and friends.

Smella, Janice

Janice Smella likes to play with fire! As a 3x Canadian National BBQ Champion, the SmellaQue Competition BBQ Team (also known as her family) travels across North America, sleeps, and hangs out in parking lots, all to spend a weekend barbecuing! Her husband cooks and their kids, too! By weekday, she's a normal gal in the office, writing contracts and going to meetings. On the weekends, Janice loves to understand the science of live fire cooking. Perfecting recipes is her best day out of the office! If there's a barbecue around, you can find her there!

Smith, Kimmie

Kimmie is a co-founder/creative and style director of Athleisure Media, publisher of *Athleisure Mag*, and host/co-producer of *Athleisure Studio*, which includes the culinary podcast, *Athleisure Kitchen*. Kimmie has also been a food judge for Cochon555. She had her Mezcal Jalapeño and Tortilla Strips Chili Verde, as well as her Mexican Lime Cream, included in Brian Baumgartner's *Seriously Good Chili Cookbook*! She is a celebrity fashion stylist and TV personality, and has been quoted in *Luxury Daily, Vogue Italia*, Today.com, *The Zoe Report*, and more! Twitter/X: @ShesKimmie @AthleisureMag; Instagram/Threads: @Shes.Kimmie @AthleisureMag; Facebook: @sheskimmie @athleisuremag

Soo, Harry

Harry Soo is a Texas Tech alumnus and an accidental pitmaster after he accepted a challenge to cook in a barbecue contest (his coworkers had recently seen the movie *The Bucket List* with Morgan Freeman and Jack Nicholson). He has won many awards and has been on Food Network, *Chopped*, and *BBQ Pitmaster*. Follow Harry on social media at @slapyodaddybbq.com!

Stachyra, Paula

Paula Stachyra, aka Queen of the Grill, is an award-winning barbecue chef, author of *Wing Crush: 100 Epic Recipes for your Grill or Smoker* and *The Big Book of Barbecue on Your Pellet Grill*, media personality, grill enthusiast, recipe developer for national brands, photographer, and content creator. She is a member of the Pit Boss Grills team and has had countless media appearances showcasing her pellet grill recipes, tips, and tricks across North America. Paula became serious about grilling eight years ago when she bought her first charcoal grill, which fueled her passion for grilling even more. She grilled almost daily and learned how to smoke the perfect ribs, pork butt, brisket, tri-tip, and spatchcock chicken, among other things. Two years after she bought her first grill, Paula added a pellet grill to her arsenal and never looked back. Throughout the years, she's added several more pellet grills to her backyard barbecue garage. She challenged herself to master the pellet grill, cooking on it daily to gain the basic knowledge of how it worked and what worked.

Sterner, Hilda

Hilda Sterner is a cookbook author and has been a food blogger since 2017 at hildaskitchenblog.com. She enjoys all kinds of dishes, but some of the most popular recipes on her blog are her smoker recipes. From smoked chicken thighs to burgers and ribs, her readers love them all!

The Korean BBQ Chef

Barbecue, specifically Korean barbecue, is a part of The Korean BBQ Chef's family's culture and traditions. When their family came to the US, they brought their recipes with them because without them, they would be like a body without a soul. As Korean Americans, they have grown up grilling meats at the dinner table, and grilled meat, such as fresh pork belly, is highly popular and the most consumed agricultural product in South Korea (even more than rice)!

Vanbecelaere, Simon

Simon Vanbecelaere's passion for barbecue and photography sparked a journey uniquely intertwined with his main profession in a psychiatric hospital. The need for a positive counterbalance led him to the world of fire cooking, where every sizzle and aroma becomes an experience. As a psychologist, Simon recognizes the importance of moments of joy. Sharing his own stories and adventures, he aims to inspire others to create more moments of pleasure and great food. This convergence of passions serves as his personal recipe for a well-rounded life, blending the art of fire-cooked cuisine with the art of nurturing the mind.

Vergos, Charlie

For over 75 years, the Vergos family has been serving their signature dry rub ribs in a basement through a downtown alley in Memphis. While the ribs are still their calling card, the menu has grown to include shoulder, brisket, half chicken, salads, cheese and sausage plates, and nachos. But a big part of what makes The Rendezvous special is the experience: the smoky aroma is grilled meat and barbecue shake. The sounds of Memphis soul and Delta blues, cut with clinking beer mugs and laughter. The taste—a perfectly seasoned Southern heaven. An experience you can only find at the world-famous Charlie Vergos Rendezvous in Memphis. It's a legendary experience whether dining in, taking out, shipping across the country, or catering an event.

Watters, Douglas

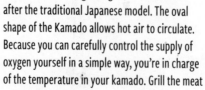

As a Southerner, Douglas Watters is a longtime barbecue and cocktail enthusiast. These days, the majority of his cocktail creations are nonalcoholic. In 2020, Douglas opened America's first booze-free bottle shop, Spirited Away. As a retailer of nonalcoholic spirits, wines, and beers, he's sampled and experimented with hundreds of products. In 2023, he launched Dry Atlas, a media company on a mission to demystify the alcohol alternatives category. Douglas spent 2023 to 2024 traveling the globe—Europe, Asia, and Central America—in search of the best nonalcoholic options worldwide, while running his two businesses.

Wilcox, Kim

Kim Wilcox is a renowned chef, cookbook author, and restaurant owner of the family-owned and operated It's All So Yummy restaurant in Knoxville, Tennessee. Kim's restaurant has been featured on the Food Network, the Cooking Channel, and local news programs. She is also the author of *Comfort Food Essentials* and *Great Book of Grilled Cheese*.

YAKINIKU

YAKINIKU® was born out of passion for fire and grilling. The YAKINIKU, which means "grilled meat" in Japanese, is the best Kamado grill, right after the traditional Japanese model. The oval shape of the Kamado allows hot air to circulate. Because you can carefully control the supply of oxygen yourself in a simple way, you're in charge of the temperature in your kamado. Grill the meat at a high temperature and let it cook further at a low temperature.

York, Jon

Jon York is a third-generation restaurant owner and a self-taught barbecue pit master. Along with his family, he has been running a family-owned barbecue joint for five years now. They specialize in pulled pork and sauces, but most recently, they took home a world champion chicken wing trophy from Memphis in May 2023.

Zimmerman, Dylan

Dylan Zimmerman also goes by Rio Good BBQ, which is his competition barbecue team name and social media handle. He started to barbecue at a young age and has always had a passion for it. When COVID hit and he was at home, Dylan would look up recipes and try to perfect them. He came across competition-style ribs and fell in love with the technique. He started his social media accounts to share his passion for barbecue with others and it led him down this road he's now on—it truly has changed his life. Meeting all the great people in the barbecue community has showed him not only how to be a better cook, but also how to be a better person.

INDEX

Note: Page numbers in *italics* indicate recipes. Page numbers in **bold** indicate contributor bios. Recipe titles followed by an asterisk (*) indicate Vegetarian dishes.

COMMON BARBECUE MEAT CUTS

BEEF RIBS

Standing Rib

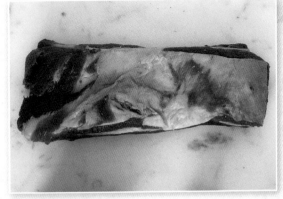

Flat Rib/Thin Rib

Wing Rib

Beef ribs are the barbecue connoisseur's choice for a hearty meal. They excel when slow-smoked until the robust meat falls off the bone.

BEEF CUTS

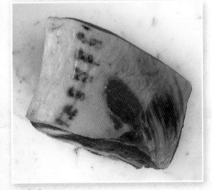

Brisket

A classic barbecue cut, known for being slow-cooked to achieve tenderness.

Chuck

Often used for burgers and also for pulled beef, given its rich marbling.

Prime Rib

Prime rib is well-suited for slow roasting, as its ample marbling renders down to create a tender and juicy cut.

T-Bone Steak

A T-bone steak offers a combination of textures from its two distinct cuts (strip steak and filet mignon), making it a great contender for barbecuing, as it's a juicy and tender cut.

Tri-Tip

Tri-tip, a triangular cut from the bottom sirloin, is excellent for barbecuing, offering a rich flavor and tender texture when cooked properly.

PORK CUTS

Pork Belly
It can be used to make deliciously crispy pork belly burnt ends, a staple of Kansas City-style barbecue.

Pork Shoulder
Pork shoulder, known for its marbling and connective tissue, becomes exceptionally tender and flavorful when slow-cooked, making it perfect for barbecue.

Spareribs
Spareribs, taken from the belly side of the rib cage, offer a meaty and flavorful barbecue experience, ideal for slow-cooking until tender.

CHICKEN

BEEF

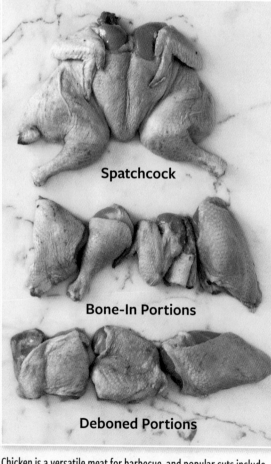

Spatchcock

Bone-In Portions

Deboned Portions

Sausage
Sausage is an essential part of barbecue and is versatile, with numerous regional varieties.

Ground Beef
Most commonly used for burgers.

Chicken is a versatile meat for barbecue, and popular cuts include spatchcocked (top), bone-in portions (middle), or deboned portions (bottom).